veggie kids

healthy, tasty dishes children will love

veggie kids

healthy, tasty dishes children will love

Roz Denny

METRO BOOKS
NEW YORK

METRO BOOKS
New York

An Imprint of Sterling Publishing
387 Park Avenue South
New York, NY 10016

METRO BOOKS and the distinctive Metro Books logo are
trademarks of Sterling Publishing Co., Inc.

© 2012 by Anness Publishing Ltd
Illustrations © 2012 by Anness Publishing Ltd

This 2010 edition published by Metro Books, by arrangement with Anness Publishing Ltd

Publisher: Joanna Lorenz
Project Editors: Zoe Antoniou and Elizabeth Young
Contributing Editor: Jenni Fleetwood
Designer: Julie Francis

ISBN: 978-1-4351-2062-4

For information about custom editions, special sales, and premium and corporate purchases, please contact
Sterling Special Sales at 800-805-5489 or specialsales@sterlingpublishing.com.

Manufactured in China

10 9 8 7 6 5 4 3 2

www.sterlingpublishers.com

COPYRIGHT HOLDER'S NOTE
Although the advice and information in this book are believed to be accurate and true at
the time of going to press, neither the authors nor the publisher can accept any legal responsibility
or liability for any errors or omissions that may be made nor for any inaccuracies nor for any
harm or injury that comes about from following instructions or advice in this book.

This book is aimed at parents cooking for their children. Many recipes, however, can be
cooked by children, and if so, make sure that they observe hygiene and safety practice
in the kitchen and are supervised at all times.

Warning: Some recipes contain nuts.

NOTES
Standard spoon and cup measures are level.
Large eggs are used unless otherwise stated.
Electric oven temperatures in this book are for conventional ovens.
When using a fan oven, the temperature will probably need to be reduced by about 20–40°F.
Since ovens vary, you should check with your manufacturer's instruction book for guidance.

Manufacturer: Anness Publishing Ltd, Hermes House, 88–89 Blackfriars Road, London SE1 8HA, England
For Product Tracking Go To: www.annesspublishing.com/tracking
Batch: 2760-22256-0095

Contents

Introduction

What do you do when your child suddenly announces that he or she has become a vegetarian? Continue to cook as you always have, but introduce more pasta and extra portions of vegetables? Hurry to the nearest store to scour the chiller cabinet for vegetarian ready-made meals? Or embrace the opportunity to introduce the whole family to a range of delicious new dishes?

If you are a vegetarian yourself, the problem will be less acute. You will already know all about the benefits of a vegetarian diet, and will doubtless have a repertoire of favorite recipes. However, what appeals to adults doesn't necessarily appeal to children, especially when they go to school and encounter what every parent dreads—peer pressure.

The child who invites friends over to eat wants to be sure that what's on the table will prove popular. That's where this book comes in. It is packed with great and tasty ideas for every occasion, from after-school snacks and treats to light lunches and more substantial family meals. The emphasis is on color, texture, and above all flavor: food that looks and tastes good, and is well-balanced and nutritious as well. But not forgetting the odd treat. Even committed meat-eaters will find these vegetarian recipes interesting and enjoyable. If cooking for a vegetarian child starts off seeming like a challenge, it will rapidly become a bonus!

You will find an array of fabulous dishes for kids of all ages in this recipe book, which is packed full of ideas for fun and delicious meals that can be achieved with ease. Each is illustrated by a beautiful color photograph of the finished dish, and the step-by-step instructions are so simple and straightforward that even a beginner will find them easy to follow. The chapters range from soups and snacks which include delights such as See-in-the-Dark Soup and Cheese Straws, to simple main meals such as Bean Burgers and Ratatouille Rumbletum. There are also tempting desserts and cakes to try to, such as Pancake Flips and Gingerbread Jungle, all of which will delight any hungry child. With so many mouthwatering recipes to choose from, there's bound to be one that will hit the right spot!

Children and Vegetarianism

It is the nutritional aspect of vegetarian food that often worries parents the most, especially non-vegetarian parents whose children have chosen not to include meat in their diet. However, with practice and awareness, meat-free meals can be balanced and healthy, as well as being every bit as appealing and easy to prepare as dishes with meat and fish.

Below: A diet rich in fresh fruit and vegetables is a key factor in living a long and healthy life. Try to consume a variety of different colored fruits and vegeables each day.

Food Appeal

Whether a child is being introduced to vegetarianism, or they have exercised a choice over what they eat, parents can ensure that everyone in the family benefits by enjoying a more varied, interesting and nutritious diet that can be very delicious.

Vegetarian children tend to be quite adventurous with trying new and different food. Encourage them to try and taste as many as you can by taking them with you when you go shopping. Children love to see the different foods available. Food stores have wonderful displays of exotic fruits and unusual vegetables, and the child who picks out a pomegranate or insists you buy a butternut squash is unlikely to refuse to try it when you get home, especially if he or she helps with the cooking.

Vegetarian food is colorful. Preparing it can be a pleasure in itself—all those greens and reds and yellows—and there's an added advantage in that much of it can be cooked quickly, so children who rapidly run out of patience can sit down to a delicious meal only moments after seeing it prepared. A stir-fry, with their favorite vegetables, is an ideal way to start. If food is fun, and children look forward to mealtimes, you will seldom have difficulty persuading them to tuck in.

Ready-made Meals

Sometimes it can be easier—and more convenient—to resort to heating up a ready-prepared meal. A word of warning, however. Many vegetarian convenience foods can be high in fat and sugar, so make sure that you check the labels carefully.

Watch out for cheese, too. It is tempting for parents of new vegetarians to think that by piling on grated cheese they are increasing their child's protein intake. What you will find is that you will also be piling on the calories too!

Eggs make a good snack as you can whip up a plate of scrambled eggs and slices of toasted whole-wheat bread in minutes. But it is worth noting that eggs should also be used in moderation—no more than four or five a week.

Exercise

Appetites are keener if a child is active. Children should not only be eating the right sorts of foods, they should be using them up in healthy ways, too. If food gives energy, that energy should be utilized; otherwise it will turn to excess body fat. A daily diet that is well-balanced will promote healthy hair, strong teeth and bones and give children a general zest for life. The child who enjoys regular exercise will develop a strong body. Team games are valuable, but so are individual activities, like swimming, cycling and walking.

Much of this advice applies to all children and not just those who are vegetarian. And that's the point. Vegetarian children are not rare or exotic beings with unusual or difficult eating habits: they are just children who choose not to eat meat. Accommodating their needs should be a pleasure, not a penance.

Above: Trying to get your children to eat vegetables can be difficult at first, but do persevere. A dish of cooked pasta with chunks of chopped broccoli and tomatoes mixed with a creamy sauce is a simple and nutritious way to get your children eating vegetables. Alternatively, for a quick snack after a busy day out or after school, you could slice up some red or green bell peppers and serve with home-made hummus.

Right: Try to get the whole family involved in regular exercise. It is good to get everyone involved in the same activity. You will help to motivate each other and it is a fun way to spend time together. Running, playing tennis or football outdoors are just a few ideas to try! Remember to have some bottles of water or fruit juice nearby, and some healthy snacks for after, such as sliced carrot sticks or fruit.

Below: Swimming is another enjoyable way to exercise with all the family. If you're lucky enough to live in a warm climate then the beaches are perfect. But if like most of us, the weather conditions are not ideal or practical for outdoor swims, then leisure centers and pools are just as good. You may even find a pool that offers water slides and a wave machine too!

A Question of Balance

A vegetarian child, if fed a balanced diet, will grow up just as healthy and strong as a child who regularly eats animal protein foods.

Energy and Nutrition

A growing child—vegetarian or not—should have a varied intake of all the nutrients necessary for maintaining good health. In effect, this means a combination of protein foods (for building and repairing body tissue), carbohydrates and, to a lesser extent, fats (for energy); minerals and vitamins (for regulating the body's chemical processes and metabolism) and sufficient fiber-rich foods to promote a good digestive system.

Each meal should have a generous proportion of carbohydrates in the form of bread, potatoes, rice or pasta. Active children have lots of energy and need adequate amounts of

Below: The range of fresh fruit and vegetables available to us throughout the year is now huge—thanks to quick transport methods. As well as buying local produce, more exotic items like baby corn, avocado and papaya can be found in supermarkets.

starchy foods to stoke them up. Sugar gives energy too, but nothing else, so while an active youngster may gain an energy boost from the occasional candy bar, these should be limited, especially as sugar is the major source of tooth decay.

Fruit and vegetables are very important sources of nutrition. Current guidelines—for children and adults—recommend five portions a day, which can include frozen vegetables as well as pure fruit juices. Try to leave edible skins on, where possible.

We all need only moderate amounts of protein. In the case of vegetarian children, protein can be obtained from dairy foods, nuts, pulses and—in small amounts—from starchy foods such as pasta. Proteins are made up of a complex combination of substances called amino acids, sometimes referred to as 'the building blocks of life' because their essential function is forming new tissue. Because vegetarian

children do not eat animal protein foods, which have all the amino acids present, it is important that they eat a variety of protein foods at each meal. One way of doing this is to combine peas or beans (or nuts, seeds or dairy products) with starchy foods in the same meal, as when serving bean burgers in wholemeal buns, or baked jacket potatoes with cheese.

The diet of a vegetarian child can be deficient in iron, so it is important to make sure your child has good vegetable sources of iron, such as spinach or other leafy green vegetables. Dried apricots

Left: Great for snacks and sandwiches, and alongside lunch and dinner, bread is full of protein, vitamins and minerals. Choose whole-wheat breads and rolls and enjoy the healthy benefits of a high fiber diet.

Above: Milk makes a delicious and nutritious drink, and is very important for the development of strong, healthy bones in babies and young children.

Below A selection of some popular dried peas and beans includes (clockwise from left), black-eyed peas, chickpeas and kidney beans.

and prunes are good sources of iron, too, as are wholegrain cereals. Breakfast cereals or bread are fortified with iron, so obtaining adequate amounts is not difficult. However, iron from a vegetable or fruit source needs to be combined with vitamin C if it is to be absorbed properly, so it is a good idea to add a tomato, orange or glass of fruit juice to the meal. Both iron and calcium are very important for growing children, not only to build a strong skeleton and help them grow tall and upright, but also to help to prevent brittle bone problems in old age.

What you have to limit with children (as with adults) is the intake of fats and sugary foods. The number of fat cells in our bodies is determined during childhood. Very plump babies can grow into overweight toddlers and may continue to have weight problems well into adult life. However, it is not desirable to feed toddlers and pre-school children low-fat foods. They need the extra vitamins found in whole milk, for example.

Achieving a balanced diet for your vegetarian child doesn't have to be difficult. Just serve a variety of foods with the emphasis on carbohydrate, and the rest will look after itself. An excellent breakfast choice would be cereal with milk, plus toast and yeast extract or peanut butter, served with a glass of fruit juice. Pasta is the perfect choice for a simple lunch, served with a tasty sauce made from pulses and vegetables, followed by a fresh fruit or a milky custard. For the evening meal, eggs on toast would be ideal, followed by a fruit yogurt.

Right: Having meals together can help to establish good eating patterns.

Fats, Sugar and Snacking

Some children prefer not to eat three full meals a day, and would rather eat a lot of small snacks more frequently. This is fine, as long as they eat the right foods in the correct proportions and not too many sugary candies, cookies or chocolates. What matters is that they are taking in a good balance of nutrients—so if you have children who love pasta dishes and fresh bread, but dislike rice and potatoes, give them the carbohydrates they crave. Equally, if a child loves apples and bananas, but dislikes certain vegetables, do not force the issue—capitalize on the favorites and introduce new tastes gradually. With so many fruits around, you will find something that will be accepted.

As snacks, offer milky drinks, diluted fruit juices, fresh fruit, nuts, dried fruits, raw vegetables such as carrots, and an occasional treat such as a chocolate bar or a couple of cookies.

Babies and Salt

Children acquire their sense of taste as babies. Tiny babies cannot cope with salt—it poisons their kidneys. Also, they have very acute taste-buds, so what may taste bland to us will be full of flavor to a baby. Never season food or feed a baby crisps or highly flavored packaged food. Nor is there a need to sprinkle boiled eggs with salt or add salt to vegetables. There is enough natural salt in fresh foods.

Ingredients for Vegetarian Kids

There are countless healthy and delicious foods that are popular with vegetarian children, including many tried and tested favorites, so you need never be short of meal ideas.

Salad Ingredients ▼
Included here are cucumbers, tomatoes (below), sweet bell peppers of all colors, celery, chicory and mushrooms. These also make good snacks for children and contribute vitamins C and B. There are many types of salad leaves such as lettuce and rocket which are also delicious when added to sandwiches.

Onion and Garlic ▼
There are lots of types of onions available, including small, sweet shallots, standard white onions, red onions, tender leeks, long, mild scallions, and thin green chives. Garlic (below) can be roasted whole, or peeled and finely chopped or grated to be added raw to dips or cooked in other dishes.

Fruit ▲
For the best flavor, value and quality, buy seasonal fruits from your supermarket. Encourage children to eat lots of fruit and drink pure fruit juices without added sugar. Bananas have valuable minerals and provide plenty of energy. Apples, pears (above), oranges, peaches and pineapple chunks are all popular, as well as some exotic fruits.

Flowers and Pods ▶
Cruciferous vegetables like cauliflower and broccoli are healthy and delicious. Add raw cauliflower to salads or eat with dips. Green beans, peas and broad beans are high in protein and carbohydrates as well as minerals. Snowpeas (right) are a delicious and colorful addition to stir-fries. They can be eaten whole and raw, or very lightly steamed for just a minute.

Leafy Green Vegetables ▲
These are excellent sources of iron, together with folic acid, vitamin C and the B group vitamins. Choose from crisp green cabbages, brussels sprouts, spinach (above), kale and curly kale, Chinese greens, and the darker green lettuces. There are many types and all are good for you. They can be eaten in a number of ways—steamed, stir-fried or boiled.

Root Vegetables ▼
Carrots are great raw as crunchy crudités or grated in salads, or they can be cooked and added to stews or soups. But children also love sweet parsnips, beets and turnips, particularly if introduced at an early age. Potatoes are filling and can be cooked in many ways. Sweet potatoes (below) and yams are also delicious, especially roasted, and they cook quickly too.

Squashes ▼
It may be the interesting shapes, the bright colors or the mild-tasting, sweet flesh, but whatever the reason, children love squashes. Introduce them to butternut (below) and acorn squashes, zucchini, large zucchini and pumpkin. They can be cut up, baked or boiled, and are delicious when used in soups, risottos and pies.

Milk and Butter ▼

Children's diets should always include milk in some form, for vitamins and calcium as well as for protein.

From the age of five, children can be given half-fat dairy produce, but younger children need whole milk (below). Butter and spreads have varying fat levels and should be served in moderation.

Tofu and Quorn ▼

A source of high class protein, tofu (below) or soya bean curd doesn't have much flavor in itself, but blends well with other foods. Quorn is a manufactured textured product made from a type of mushroom. It has a bland flavor but is very versatile. Both are very useful ingredients if you want to prepare a quick and healthy meal.

Pulses and beans ▼

Packed with good quality protein with very little fat, pulses are also valuable sources of dietary fiber, vitamins and minerals. Kidney beans, chickpeas and lentils (below) tend to be the most popular varieties.

Don't forget those great stand-bys: baked beans, hummus and all the soya bean products.

Rice ▼

There are several different types of rice, including long grain rice, easy-cook rice, brown rice, basmati rice, paella rice, risotto rice, jasmine rice and pudding rice. It's important to use the one mentioned in the recipe, because they look, taste and feel different when cooked, and also take different amounts of time to cook.

Cheese ▼

From hard, strong varieties, such as Cheddar, and Parmesan to soft, mild ones, such as brie or creamy marscarpone, cheese can be used in all kinds of savory and sweet dishes. Some, such as Cheddar or mozzarella, are perfect for melting, while others, such as feta or halloumi, are better crumbled or sliced and served raw or just lightly cooked.

Nuts and Seeds ▼

These are sources of good quality protein and there are many different varieties to tempt and please children. Almonds, hazelnuts, cashews (below), pistachios, and macadamia nuts are all delicious. Sprinkle sunflower seeds over salads and add sesame seeds to breads and cakes as these are also a good source of calcium.

Pasta ▼

One of the quickest and easiest things to cook, there are two main types of pasta—fresh and dried, and these can be standard or whole-wheat. They come in many shapes and sizes. Cook all types according to the packet instructions, in a large pan of lightly salted boiling water. Then simply add your favorite sauce and tuck in!

Bread ▼

Starchy foods such as bread should form at least half of the calorie intake of any good diet. Bread gives children energy for growth and everyday activities. So make the most of toast, sandwiches and even the pizza.

Parents of children with gluten or wheat allergies should check labels carefully. Use gluten-free and non-wheat flours.

Meal Planning

Children can be quite conservative when it comes to menu choices, so encourage them to experiment by balancing the courses for them. Seeing you take care when it comes to combining colors, textures and flavors also helps them to understand that food is not just for eating, it's for enjoyment as well. In time, it will become second nature for them to balance their own meals, teaming a strongly flavored dish with a milder or creamier one, and creating contrasts by following a creamy potato-topped pie with a crisp, fruity dessert. All the meal choices that follow come from the book, but you can mix and match. If you are ever stuck for a pudding, just slice up two or three fruits in a bowl and trickle over a little yogurt and some clear honey.

Chili Cheese Nachos ▲　　　**Wicked Tortilla Wedges ▲**

Contrary to popular opinion, many children like spicy food, as long as it is mild. So, treat them to a Mexican-Spanish meal. Nachos make an unusual starter; the main-meal omelette is packed full of wholesome vegetables and is cut in wedges for serving. Great with a tomato or green salad.

Corn and Potato Chowder ▲　　　**Pitta Pizzas ▲**

A chunky soup with lots of fresh vegetables works well as a prelude to quick and easy pizzas made with pitta breads. The soup is rich in beans—and vegetable protein. There is no need to serve the pizza with the extra toppings suggested—for this menu it is complete as it is.

Broccoli Bubble ▲　　　**Lazy Pastry Pudding ▲**

Broccoli Bubble is a variation on that family favorite, cauliflower cheese. Topped with a funny face, it's the perfect dish to tempt reluctant eaters. When making the pudding, get your child to help make the pastry and peel and slice the apples. It's as easy as pie!

Bean Burgers ▲

Carrot Salad ▲

Tofu and Vegetable Stir-fry ▲

Rice Pudding ▲

The burgers stand up well in comparison to hamburgers, so are a good choice for after-school meals. Make up a batch and freeze some for later. The carrot salad, with its lemon dressing, can either be served as a starter or as an accompaniment.

If your children haven't yet tried tofu, this is an excellent recipe to try. Colorful and full of flavor and contrasting textures, this stir-fry appeals to all ages, and is, incidentally, an excellent choice for students cooking on a single burner. Follow it with a creamy rice pudding.

Soft Cheese and Chive Dip ▲

Vegetable Paella ▲

Hummus ▲

Calzone ▲

Children enjoy dips and this one is a sure success. Serve it with breadsticks or sticks of their favorite salad vegetables or cauliflower florets. To follow, try a vegetarian version of the Spanish classic—an easy all-in-one dish based on rice, vegetables and pulses.

Hummus is made from a purée of protein-rich chickpeas, and is popular with many children. It is excellent served with lightly fried zucchini, or carrot sticks. Calzone is really a folded pizza, with all the usual healthy ingredients but a more interesting package!

Techniques

Chopping Onions

Evenly diced onions will cook quickly and easily. Use a sharp knife and mind your fingers!

1 Peel the onion. Cut it in half with a large knife and set it cut-side down on a board. Make lengthwise vertical cuts along the onion, cutting almost but not quite through to the root.

2 Make two horizontal cuts from the stalk and towards the root, but not through it. Cut the onion crosswise to form small, even dice.

Thinly Slicing Vegetables

Here is a simple way of slicing vegetables safely. Slice potatoes, parsnips or carrots this way.

1 Peel the vegetables as required. Take a thin slice off one side, to give a solid base to stand on and prevent it from sliding around.

2 Stand the vegetable on its flat base and slice thinly with a sharp knife. Keep your fingers tucked away, using your knuckles as a guide.

Making Vegetable Stock

Vegetable stock is easy to make and doesn't take very long, so it is worth making a reasonable amount and freezing the surplus.

Makes 5 cups

INGREDIENTS
2 onions
2 carrots
2 large celery stalks, plus any small
    amounts from the following:
    leeks, celery root, parsnips, turnips,
    cabbage, cauliflower and mushrooms
2 tbsp vegetable oil
bouquet garni
7½ cups cold water
ground black pepper

1 Peel, halve and slice the onions. Wash, peel, if preferred, and coarsely chop all the remaining vegetables into medium sized pieces.

2 Heat the oil in a large pan and sauté the onion and vegetables until soft and lightly browned. Add the bouquet garni and pepper.

3 Cover with the water and bring to the boil. Skim the surface, then partially cover and leave to simmer gently for 1½ hours. Allow to cool. Strain the stock into a large pitcher and discard the vegetables and pour the stock into a pitcher. It is now ready to use.

COOK'S TIP
Freeze the stock in ice-cube trays. That way you can reheat only as much as you actually need.

Cooking Long Grain Brown Rice

The nutritional bran coating in brown rice creates a nutty flavor and chewy texture.

Serves 4

INGREDIENTS
1 cup long grain brown rice
plenty of boiling water, approx.
  5¼ cups

VARIATION
This is the open pan/fast boiling method, where the rice is covered in plenty of water. For the covered pan/absorption method, a specific amount of water is required and the rice is cooked when this has been absorbed. If in doubt, follow the instructions on the packet.

1 Put the rice in a large pan and cover with the boiling water. If you want to cook much more rice, you just need to make sure that the rice is covered with plenty of water.

2 Stir the rice, to break up the grains, then bring back to the boil. Lower the heat and simmer, uncovered, for about 35 minutes, until the grains are tender but firm to the bite.

3 Drain the rice through a strainer, then rinse it well with fresh boiling water to remove the starch. Serve immediately.

COOK'S TIP
Brown rice gives a more sustaining energy than white rice.

Cooking Pasta

Depending on the age of the children (and how hungry they are) allow about 1 cup dried pasta per person if it is the main ingredient, and a little less if it is to accompany a meal.

Serves 4

INGREDIENTS
3–4 cups dried pasta
pinch of salt

VARIATION
Fresh pasta is widely available. It cooks much more quickly than dried: as a general rule, it will be ready as soon as it rises to the top of the liquid in which it is boiled.

1 Bring a large pan of water to the boil. Stir in a little salt. Add the pasta to the pan, a little at a time, so that the water stays at a rolling boil and the pasta does not stick together.

2 Cook for 8–12 minutes, depending on the type of pasta – spaghetti will not take as long as the thicker penne pasta. Be guided by the time on the packet. It should be al dente when cooked, which means it still has some firmness to it and isn't completely soft and soggy.

3 Drain the pasta well in a colander and tip it back into the pan. Pour a sauce over it or toss in a little melted butter or olive oil. Serve immediately.

COOK'S TIP
Always stir pasta once it has started to cook so that the pieces don't stick.

Making Mayonnaise

Because it contains raw yolks, it is important to use only fresh eggs from a reputable source for home-made mayonnaise. Even so, it is best not to serve this to young children. It is certainly delicious, though, and is fun to make.

Makes about 1¼ cups

INGREDIENTS
2 egg yolks
1 tsp French mustard
⅔ cup extra-virgin olive oil
⅔ cup sunflower oil
2 tsp white wine vinegar
salt and ground black pepper

COOK'S TIP
If mayonnaise separates during blending, add 2 tbsp boiling water and beat until smooth. Store mayonnaise in the fridge for up to 1 week, sealed in a screw-top jar.

1 Put the egg yolks and mustard in a food processor and blend smoothly.

2 Add the olive oil a little at a time through the feeder tube, while the processor is running. When the mixture is thick, add the sunflower oil in a slow steady stream.

3 Add the vinegar and season to taste with salt and pepper.

Making Salad Dressing

Green or mixed salads add crunch and freshness to hearty meals like vegetable lasagne or bean pot, but they can be bland and boring without a dressing like this one, which children can easily make themselves.

Serves 4

INGREDIENTS
1 tbsp white wine vinegar
2 tsp coarse-grain mustard
2 tbsp sunflower oil
salt and ground black pepper

COOK'S TIP
For a tangy dressing, mix 2 tbsp oil with 1 tbsp lemon juice. Add chopped fresh herbs for extra flavour.

1 Put the vinegar and mustard in a bowl or pitcher. Whisk well, then add a little salt and pepper.

2 Add the oil slowly, about 1 tsp at a time, whisking all the time with a whisk or a fork. Pour the dressing over the salad just before serving so that the lettuce stays crisp. Use two spoons to toss the salad and coat it with the dressing.

Preparing Mango Hedgehogs

Removing the stone and skin from a mango can be done in three easy steps, and the results look as impressive as they taste.

Peeling a Pineapple

Try this clever all-in-one way of removing the peel from a fresh pineapple.

1 Holding the mango upright on a chopping board, use a large knife to slice the flesh away from either side of the large flat stone in two pieces. Use a smaller knife to trim away the flesh still clinging to the stone.

2 Score the flesh of the mango halves deeply, taking care to avoid cutting through the skin; make parallel incisions approximately ½ in apart, then turn the mango half round and cut lines in the opposite direction.

3 Carefully turn the skin inside out so that the flesh stands out like the prickles of a hedgehog. To eat, slice the diced flesh away from the skin.

1 Using one hand to hold the pineapple firmly on a board, cut off the leafy top with a large sharp knife.

COOK'S TIP
Children should be taught how to use knives safely and should never be left unsupervised in the kitchen.

2 Cutting at a 45° angle, make an incision in the pineapple skin, following the natural diagonal line of the eyes. When you reach the end of the line, turn the pineapple over and cut the other side of the line of eyes in the same way. Pull off the strip of skin.

3 Continue cutting the skin of the pineapple in the same way until it is completely peeled, then slice or chop as required in recipes.

Instant Dips

Children of all ages find dips irresistible, and they are a marvelous vehicle for sticks of carrot, celery, cucumber or colorful mixed bell peppers. Raw mushrooms, radishes and blanched broccoli and cauliflower florets can be used as dippers too, providing a perfect way of persuading kids who claim to hate salad to eat fresh vegetables.

Cheese straws

Bread sticks

Vegetable crudités

Fruit crudités

Vegetable crisps

Tortilla chips

Corn chips

Potato chips

Creamy black olive dip

To make a great dip for bread sticks, stir a little black olive paste into a carton of extra thick double cream until smooth and well blended. Add salt and pepper and a squeeze of fresh lemon juice to taste. Serve chilled. For a low-calorie version, substitute low-fat natural or strained plain yogurt for the cream. This is a great dip for adults too, and would be a unique and delightgul surprise at a dinner party.

Crème fraîche or sour cream with scallions

Finely chop a bunch of scallions and stir into a carton of crème fraîche or sour cream. Add a dash of mild chili sauce, a squeeze of fresh lime juice and a little salt and ground black pepper to taste. For children who don't like chili sauce, stir in a fruity chutney instead. Serve with tortilla chips or alongside a spicy guacamole. This will also make a tasty topping for a baked potato.

Yogurt and mustard dip

Mix a small carton of creamy strained plain yogurt with one or two teaspoons of mild wholegrain mustard. Serve with breadsticks or vegetable dippers. Not only does it make a superb and healthy savory snack, it will also appeal to children who may find plain yogurt a little bland.

Herby mayonnaise

Liven up ready-made mayonnaise, or a delicious home-made version, with a handful of your favorite chopped fresh herbs—try flat-leaf parsley, basil, dill or tarragon. Season lightly and serve with crisp carrot and cucumber batons or cheese straws.

Passata and horseradish dip

Teenagers like this one—bring a little tang to a small carton or bottle of strained tomatoes by adding some horseradish sauce or a teaspoon or two of creamed horseradish. Stir in salt and pepper to taste and serve with vegetable or spicy tortilla chips.

Pesto dip

For a simple, speedy Italian-style dip, stir a tablespoon of ready-made red or green pesto into a carton of soured cream. Serve with crisp crudités or wedges of oven-roasted Mediterranean vegetables, such as peppers, zucchini and onions.

Farmer's cheese and chive dip

Mix a tub of farmer's cheese with two or three tablespoons of snipped fresh chives and season to taste with salt and plenty of black pepper. If the dip is a little too thick, stir in a spoonful or two of milk to soften it. This is a great dip if you don't want a spicy one.

Spiced yogurt dip

To make a speedy Indian-style dip, stir a little mild curry paste into a carton of natural yogurt. Add a finely chopped apple or a spoonful or two of mango chutney and serve with crisp poppadoms or corn chips.

Yogurt and sun-dried tomato dip

Stir one or two tablespoons of sun-dried tomato paste into a carton of strained plain yogurt. Season lightly and serve with small triangles of crisp toasted pitta bread. Soured cream or even low-fat fromage frais can be used instead of yogurt, if you like.

Creamy black
olive dip

Crème fraîche
with scallions

Herby mayonnaise

Yogurt and sun-dried
tomato dip

Yogurt and mustard dip

Farmer's
cheese and
chive dip

Pesto dip

Spiced yogurt dip

Tomato and
horseradish dip

Soups and Snacks

Winter Warm-up

Simmer a selection of popular winter root vegetables together for a warming and satisfying soup. Serve with crusty rolls for a complete meal.

Serves 6

INGREDIENTS
2 tbsp sunflower oil
¼ stick butter
3 medium carrots, chopped
1 large potato, chopped
1 large parsnip, chopped
1 large turnip or small rutabaga, chopped
1 onion, chopped
6¼ cups water
1 piece fresh root ginger, peeled and grated
1¼ cups milk
3 tbsp crème fraîche, fromage frais or plain yogurt
2 tbsp chopped fresh dill
salt and ground black pepper

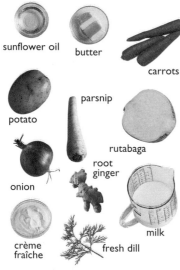

sunflower oil
butter
carrots
potato
parsnip
rutabaga
root ginger
onion
crème fraîche
fresh dill
milk

COOK'S TIP
After completing the soup, reheat it, if you like, but do not let it boil, or it may curdle.

1 Heat the oil and butter in a large pan, then add the carrots, potato, parsnip, turnip or rutabaga and onion. Fry lightly, then cover and sweat the vegetables over a very low heat for 15 minutes, shaking the pan occasionally.

2 Pour in the water, bring to the boil and season well. Lower the heat, cover and simmer for 20 minutes until the vegetables are soft.

3 Strain the vegetables, reserving the stock, and tip them into a food processor or blender. Add the ginger and purée until smooth. Return the purée and stock to the pan. Add the milk. Reheat gently, stirring all the time.

4 Remove the soup from the heat and stir in the crème fraîche, fromage frais or yogurt, plus the dill and extra seasoning, if necessary.

Corn and Potato Chowder

Children of all ages love this hearty and substantial soup. High in both fibre and flavor, it is wonderful with thick crusty bread.

Serves 4

INGREDIENTS
2 tbsp sunflower oil
1/4 stick butter
1 onion, chopped
1 garlic clove, crushed
1 medium potato, chopped
2 celery sticks, sliced
1 small green bell pepper, seeded,
   halved and sliced
2 1/2 cups vegetable stock or water
1 1/4 cups milk
7oz can wax beans
11oz can corn
good pinch of dried sage
salt and ground black pepper

sunflower oil
butter
onion
garlic
potato
celery
green bell pepper
vegetable stock
corn
wax beans
milk
dried sage

COOK'S TIP
This tastes great with a topping of grated cheese, melted under the broiler.

1 Heat the oil and butter in a large pan. Add the onion, garlic, potato, celery and green pepper and mix well.

2 Heat the vegetables in the oil mixture until sizzling, then turn the heat down to low. Cover the pan and sweat the vegetables gently for 10 minutes, shaking the pan occasionally.

3 Pour in the stock or water, season to taste and bring to the boil. Lower the heat, replace the lid and simmer gently for about 15 minutes.

4 Stir in the milk, butter beans and corn – including the liquid in the cans, then add the sage. Simmer for 5 minutes more. Check the seasoning and serve hot.

See-in-the-Dark Soup

If you want your children to stop stumbling around when the lights are off – serve them more carrots so they will be able to see in the dark! Mixed with lentils, they make a marvellous soup.

Serves 4

INGREDIENTS
1 tbsp sunflower oil
1 onion, sliced
2 cups carrots, sliced
½ cup split red lentils
5 cups vegetable stock
1 tsp ground coriander
3 tbsp chopped fresh parsley
salt and ground black pepper
toast, to serve

sunflower oil

onion

carrots

red lentils

vegetable stock

ground coriander

fresh parsley

COOK'S TIP

Serve this with toast hearts. The children can make these themselves by pressing out shapes from sliced bread with the aid of cookie cutters. Toast the hearts under the broiler or dry them out in a warm oven.

1 Heat the oil and fry the onion until it is starting to brown. Add the sliced carrots and fry gently for 4–5 minutes, stirring them often, until they soften.

2 Meanwhile, put the lentils in a bowl and cover with cold water. Pour off any bits that float, then tip them into a strainer and rinse under water.

3 Add the lentils, vegetable stock and coriander to the pan together with a little salt and pepper. Bring the soup to the boil.

4 Lower the heat, cover with a lid and leave to simmer gently for 30 minutes, or until the lentils are cooked.

5 Add the chopped parsley and cook for 5 minutes more. Remove from the heat and allow to cool slightly.

6 Purée the soup in a food processor or blender until smooth. (You may have to do this in two batches.) Rinse the pan first before pouring the soup back in and add a little water if it looks too thick. Reheat it before serving with toast.

Super-duper Soup

This soup is very easy to make – just chop up lots of your children's favorite vegetables and simmer them gently with tomatoes and stock.

Serves 4–6

INGREDIENTS
1 tbsp sunflower oil
1 onion, sliced
2 carrots, sliced
1½ lb potatoes, cut in large chunks
5 cups vegetable stock
1lb can chopped tomatoes
4oz broccoli, cut in florets
1 zucchini, sliced
1½ cups mushrooms, sliced
1½ tsp medium-hot curry powder
 (optional)
1 tsp dried mixed herbs
salt and ground black pepper

1 Heat the oil in a large pan and fry the onion and carrots gently until they start to soften and the onions are just beginning to turn light brown.

sunflower oil

onion

carrots

potatoes

vegetable stock

chopped tomatoes

zucchini

mushrooms

curry powder

broccoli florets

dried mixed herbs

COOK'S TIP
For a special treat, serve this with breadsticks. Small children love the idea of edible stirrers.

2 Add the potatoes and fry gently for 2 minutes more. Stir them gently and regularly so that they do not stick to the pan. Pour in the stock, then add the chopped tomatoes, broccoli, courgette and mushrooms.

3 Stir in the curry powder (if using), with the herbs. Season lightly and bring to the boil. Cover and simmer gently for 30–40 minutes, or until the vegetables are tender. Serve hot with slices of fresh bread, if you like.

Tasty Toasts

Finger food is perfect for kids on the go. These toasts also appeal to teenagers and siblings with sophisticated tastes.

Serves 4

INGREDIENTS
2 red bell peppers, halved lengthways and seeded
2 tbsp sunflower oil
1 garlic clove, crushed
1 short French stick
3 tbsp pesto
1/3 cup soft goat's cheese

red bell peppers

sunflower oil

garlic

French stick

pesto

soft goat's cheese

1 Put the pepper halves, cut-side down, under a hot broiler until the skins blacken, then transfer them to a plastic bag, tie the top and leave them until they are cool enough to handle. Peel off the skins and cut the peppers into strips.

2 Put the oil in a small bowl and stir in the crushed garlic. Cut the bread diagonally into slices and brush one side of each slice with the garlic-flavored oil. Arrange the bread slices on a broiling pan and brown under a hot broiler.

3 Turn the bread slices over. Brush the untoasted sides generously with the garlic-flavored oil, then spread with the pesto.

4 Arrange pepper strips over each slice and put small wedges of goat's cheese on top. Broil again until the cheese has browned and melted slightly. Serve hot or cold.

VARIATION

For children who don't like pesto, substitute home-made tomato sauce. Brown an onion in a little oil, add a can of chopped tomatoes with basil, stir in a generous squeeze from a tube of tomato purée and add a pinch of sugar. Simmer until thick and tasty.

Hummus with Pan-fried Zucchini

Pan-fried zucchini are perfect for dipping into home-made hummus.

Serves 4

INGREDIENTS
8 oz can chickpeas
2 garlic cloves, roughly chopped
6 tbsp lemon juice
4 tbsp tahini paste
5 tbsp olive oil, plus extra to serve
1 tsp ground cumin
1 lb small zucchini
salt and ground black pepper

TO SERVE
paprika (optional)
pitta bread
black olives

garlic cloves

chickpeas

tahini paste

olive oil   lemon

ground cumin   zucchini

COOK'S TIP

Hummus is also delicious served with pan-fried or broiled eggplant slices. Paprika is used here for extra color. Leave it out if the children don't like the flavor.

1 Drain the chickpeas, reserving the liquid from the can, and tip them into a food processor or blender. Blend to a smooth purée, adding a small amount of the reserved can liquid if necessary, in case it becomes too bulky and dry.

2 Mix the garlic, lemon juice and tahini together in a bowl and add to the food processor or blender. Process until smooth. With the machine running, gradually add 3 tbsp of the olive oil through the feeder tube or lid. Add the cumin, with salt and pepper to taste.

3 Process to mix, then scrape the hummus into a bowl. Cover and chill until required. Top and tail the zucchini. Slice them lengthways into even-size pieces.

4 Heat the remaining oil in a large frying pan. Fry the zucchini for 2–3 minutes on each side until just tender.

5 Divide the zucchini among four individual plates. Spoon a portion of hummus on to each plate, and sprinkle with paprika, if using. Add two or three pieces of sliced pitta bread and serve with olives.

Chili Cheese Nachos

Mexican food is the flavor of the moment. Serve this and you will be, too! Make it as cool or as hot as you like, by adjusting the amount of sliced jalapeños that are used.

Serves 4

INGREDIENTS
4oz bag chili or tortilla chips
½ cup grated Cheddar cheese
½ cup grated Red Leicester cheese
⅓ cup pickled green jalapeño
    chilies, sliced

FOR THE DIP
1 avocado, roughly chopped
1 beefsteak tomato, roughly chopped
2 tbsp lemon juice
salt and ground black pepper

1 Spread out the tortilla chips in an even layer on a plate which can safely be used under the broiler. Sprinkle with both the grated cheeses and then scatter as many jalapeño chilies as you like over the top.

tortilla chips

pickled green jalapeño chilies

lemon juice

beefsteak tomato

avocado

grated Cheddar cheese

grated Red Leicester cheese

COOK'S TIP
Seed the chilies before you slice them if you want to keep their flavor without the heat.

2 Put the plate under a hot broiler until the cheese has melted and browned, but make sure the tortilla chips don't burn.

3 Make the dip by mixing avocado, tomato and lemon juice in a bowl. Add salt and pepper to taste and serve with the chips.

Cheese Straws

These will become a family favorite. Everyone loves them, from teens to toddlers! They are so tasty you may even find them fast disappearing as soon as they have come out of the oven. They are ideal for dips, soups and snacks.

Serves 4 –6

INGREDIENTS
little oil, for greasing
1½ cups all-purpose flour
¾ stick butter or margarine,
    cut into pieces
1 cup grated Cheddar cheese
1 egg, beaten

flour   butter

egg

grated
Cheddar
cheese

oil

1 Preheat the oven to 400°F. Lightly brush two baking sheets with oil. Place the flour in a large bowl and rub in the butter or margarine.

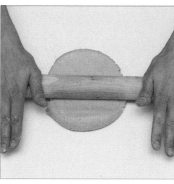

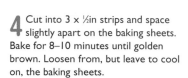

VARIATION
Spread the cheese pastry with a thin layer of yeast extract for a different version of the straws. Or, sprinkle them with grated cheese before baking for an extra cheesy taste.

2 Stir the grated Cheddar cheese into the flour mixture. Reserve 1 tbsp beaten egg for glazing and stir the rest into the mixture too. Mix to a smooth dough, adding a little water if necessary.

3 Knead lightly, then roll out on a floured surface to a 12 x 8in rectangle. Brush with the remaining beaten egg.

4 Cut into 3 x ½in strips and space slightly apart on the baking sheets. Bake for 8–10 minutes until golden brown. Loosen from, but leave to cool on, the baking sheets.

Skinny Dippers

Baked potato skins are always popular, particularly when served with a spicy dip, and these are healthier than chips. Don't over do the salt, especially if serving these to young children.

Serves 4

INGREDIENTS
8 large potatoes, scrubbed
2–3 tbsp sunflower oil
6 tbsp mayonnaise
2 tbsp plain yogurt
1 tsp curry paste
2 tbsp roughly chopped
    fresh cilantro
salt

 potatoes

 sunflower oil

mayonnaise

plain yogurt

curry paste

fresh cilantro

COOK'S TIP

For a single portion, prick one large potato all over with a fork and microwave on HIGH for 6–8 minutes, until tender. Scoop out the centre, brush with oil and broil briefly until browned.

1 Preheat the oven to 375°F. Arrange the potatoes in a roasting pan, prick them all over with a fork and cook for 1–1¼ hours, or until tender. Leave aside to cool slightly so that you can touch them more easily.

2 Protecting your hand with a dish towel, carefully cut each potato lengthways into quarters.

3 Scoop out some of the cooked potato from each skin, using a knife or spoon. Put the skins back in the roasting pan. Save the cooked potato for another snack of your choice.

4 Brush the skins with oil and sprinkle them lightly with salt before putting them back in the oven. Cook for 30–40 minutes more, until they are crisp and brown, brushing them occasionally with more oil.

5 Meanwhile, mix the mayonnaise, yogurt, curry paste and half the chopped coriander in a small bowl. Cover and leave for 30–40 minutes to allow the flavour to develop.

6 Put the dip in a clean bowl and sprinkle with the remaining coriander. Arrange the skins on a serving plate and serve hot.

Bread Zoo

Shaping these dough animals is great fun for adults and children alike. Serve hot with soup.

Makes 15

INGREDIENTS
2 x 10oz packets white bread mix
oil, for greasing
a few currants
1/2 small red bell pepper
1 small carrot
beaten egg, to glaze

bread mix

currants

carrot

egg

red bell
pepper

oil

COOK'S TIP

Bread mixes are a fast and easy way to make bread, and although you are more restricted with the types of bread you can make, the results are just as delicious. You can find mixes in most stores, and instructions for making the bread will be on the packet.

1 Put the bread mix in a large bowl and make up as directed on the packet with warm water. When it is a pliable dough, knead on a lightly floured surface for 5 minutes until the dough is smooth and elastic. Return the dough to the bowl, cover with oiled clear film and leave in a warm place for 3/4–1 hour until it has doubled in size.

2 Knead the dough again for 5 minutes and divide into five pieces. Cut one piece of dough into three and shape each into a 6in snake, making a slit for the mouth. Twist the snakes on a greased baking sheet and add currant eyes. Slice a thin strip of pepper, cutting a triangle at one end for the forked tongue.

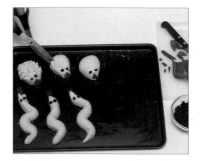

3 For hedgehogs, take another piece of dough and cut into three. Shape each into an oval about 2 1/2 in long. Place on the baking sheet and add currant eyes and a red pepper nose. Snip the dough with scissors to make the prickly spines.

4 To make mice, take a third piece of dough and cut into four pieces. Shape three pieces into ovals each about 2 1/2 in long and place on the baking sheet. Shape tiny rounds of dough for ears and wiggly tails from the fourth piece of dough. Press on to the mice bodies and use the currants for eyes, and small strips of carrot for whiskers.

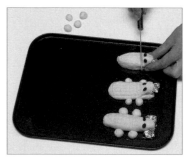

5 For crocodiles, cut another piece of dough into three. Take a small piece off each and reserve. Shape the large pieces into 4in long sausages. Make slits for the mouths and wedge open with crumpled foil. Add currant eyes. Shape the spare dough into feet and press into position. Make criss-cross cuts on the backs for scales.

6 To make rabbits, cut the final dough into three. Take a small piece off each for tails. Roll the main pieces into thick sausages, 7in long. Loop the dough and twist twice to form the body and head of the rabbit. Use the rest for tails. Preheat the oven to 425°F. Cover all with oiled clear film and leave for 12 minutes. Brush with beaten egg and cook for 10–12 minutes until golden.

Log Cabin

This takes a little time but it is a great favorite with children of all ages. You can make whatever fillings you like, which will keep everyone happy.

Serves 4

INGREDIENTS
4 whole-wheat sandwiches, each with a
    favorite filling, crusts removed
pretzel sticks
¼ cup farmer's cheese
1 tomato
1 carrot
1 radish
1 in piece cucumber

whole-wheat bread

pretzels ticks

farmer's cheese

tomato

radish

carrot

cucumber

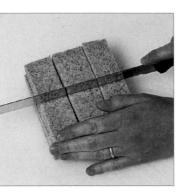

1 Place two of the sandwiches on a chopping board and cut each into small rectangles.

2 Cut each of the remaining two sandwiches diagonally to make four triangles.

3 Stack the sandwich rectangles together to form the cabin and place six of the triangles on top to form the pointed roof. (Any spare triangles can be served separately.)

4 Arrange pretzel sticks on the roof to look like logs, sticking them in place with a little sandwich filling or some farmer's cheese if necessary.

5 Break the remaining pretzel sticks into 1 in lengths and use to make a fence around the cabin, sticking them in place with farmer's cheese.

6 Cut doors and windows from the tomato, then cut a carrot wedge for the chimney, attaching it with curd cheese. Add some farmer's cheese smoke. Cut flowers from the radish and carrot. Dice the cucumber finely and arrange on the board to resemble a path.

COOK'S TIP

When making the sandwiches, choose simple, complementary fillings, such as tomato, hard-boiled egg, cheese and yeast extract. If you don't have time to make several fillings, you could make them all the same.

Spicy Spuds

Filled jacket potatoes make an excellent and nourishing meal. If you're in a hurry, microwave the potatoes. Creamed corn makes an alternative filling to chili beans.

Serves 4

INGREDIENTS
4 medium baking potatoes
olive oil, for brushing

FOR THE FILLING
15oz can red kidney beans, drained
scant 1 cup low-fat farmer's cheese or
  cream cheese
1–2 tbsp mild chili sauce
1 tsp ground cumin

1 Preheat the oven to 400°F. Score the potatoes with a deep cross and rub them all over with olive oil. Place directly on the oven shelf and cook for about an hour, or until tender.

farmer's cheese   red kidney beans

baking potatoes   ground cumin

chili sauce   olive oil

VARIATION

You don't have to flavor the filling with chili and cumin. Chutney, pickle, tomato paste or even tomato ketchup can be used instead.

COOK'S TIP

For speed, you can always cook baked potatoes in the Microwave and the end result is pretty good. Prick and score the potatoes, wrap them in kitchen towels and place in the microwave on HIGH for about 12 minutes. The more potatoes that are being cooked, the longer the cooking time.

2 When the potatoes are almost ready, prepare the filling. Heat the beans in a pan, then stir in the cheese, chili sauce and cumin.

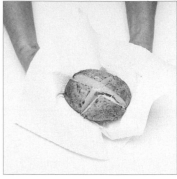

3 Cut the potatoes open along the score lines and push up the flesh from the base with your fingers. Fill with the chili bean mixture. Serve immediately while hot.

Pitta Pizzas

Pitta breads make very good bases for quick pizzas. Children are very particular when it comes to toppings, so set out a selection and let each child choose. Better still, let them top their own.

Serves 4

INGREDIENTS
4 pitta breads, ideally whole-wheat
½ cup home-made or bottled
    pasta sauce
1 cup mozzarella cheese, sliced
    or grated
dried oregano or thyme, for sprinkling
salt and ground black pepper
fresh basil, to garnish

FOR THE EXTRA TOPPINGS (OPTIONAL)
1 small red onion, thinly sliced and
    lightly fried
½ cup mushrooms, sliced and fried
7oz can corn, drained
jalapeño chilies, sliced
black or green olives, stoned and sliced
capers, drained

pitta breads

pasta sauce

mozzarella
cheese

dried thyme

fresh
basil

1 Preheat the broiler and lightly toast the pitta breads on both sides.

2 Spread pasta sauce on to each pitta, taking it right to the edge. This prevents the edges of the pitta from burning.

VARIATION
The suggested toppings are quite sophisticated. Younger children may prefer Cheddar cheese with tomato or small broccoli florets.

3 Arrange cheese slices or grated cheese on top of each pitta and sprinkle lightly with herbs and seasoning.

4 Add any extra toppings and then broil the pizzas for about 5–8 minutes until they are golden brown and bubbling. Garnish with basil and serve immediately, with a mixed leaf salad, if you like.

Broccoli Bubble

Making a face or a pattern on food can be just the thing to tempt a fussy eater to try something new.

Serves 2

INGREDIENTS
½ cup broccoli
½ cup cauliflower
¼ half stick butter or margarine
1 tbsp all-purpose flour
⅔ cup milk
⅓ cup grated Red Leicester cheese
½ tomato
1 egg, hard-boiled

broccoli   cauliflower

butter   flour   milk

grated Red Leicester cheese

hard-boiled egg

tomato

1 Cut the broccoli and cauliflower into small florets. Bring a small pan of water to the boil. Add the broccoli and cauliflower and cook for about 8 minutes until just tender. Drain and set aside.

2 Melt the butter or margarine in a pan, stir in the flour and cook for a few minutes. Gradually mix in the milk. Bring to the boil, stirring until the sauce thickens and is smooth. Stir in two-thirds of the cheese.

3 Set aside two broccoli florets and stir the remaining vegetables into the sauce. Divide the mixture between two shallow gratin dishes and sprinkle with the remaining cheese.

4 Place under a hot broiler until golden brown and bubbling. Make a face with broccoli florets for a nose, a halved tomato for a mouth and peeled and sliced hard-boiled egg for eyes. Cool slightly before serving.

COOK'S TIP

Red Leicester gives the sauce a rich color and flavor, but you can use another grating cheese if you prefer.

Chunky Cheesy Salad

Something for the children to really sink their teeth into – this salad is full of vitamins and energy.

Serves 4

INGREDIENTS
¼ small white cabbage, finely chopped
¼ small red cabbage, finely chopped
8 baby carrots, thinly sliced
½ cup small mushrooms, quartered
4oz cauliflower, cut in small florets
1 small zucchini grated
4in piece cucumber, cubed
2 tomatoes, roughly chopped
1 cup sprouted seeds
½ cup salted peanuts
2 tbsp sunflower oil
1 tbsp lemon juice
½ cup grated cheese
fresh bread, to serve

1 Put all the prepared vegetables, the tomatoes and the sprouted seeds in a bowl and mix together well.

red cabbage

white cabbage

baby carrots

mushrooms

cucumber

zucchini

tomatoes

cauliflower

sprouted seeds

peanuts

sunflower oil

lemon juice

grated cheese

COOK'S TIP

Be cautious when using peanuts. Some children are highly allergic to them. If in any doubt, leave them out.

2 Stir in the peanuts. Drizzle with oil and lemon juice. Toss lightly, then leave to stand for 30 minutes to allow the flavors to develop.

3 Sprinkle grated cheese over the salad just before serving it on large slices of crusty bread. Have extra dressing ready, in case anybody wants more.

Wicked Tortilla Wedges

A tortilla is a thick omelette with lots of cooked potatoes in it. It is very popular in Spain, where it is cut in thick slices like a cake and served with bread. Try it with sliced tomato salad.

Serves 4

INGREDIENTS
2 tbsp sunflower oil
1½lb potatoes, cut in small chunks
I onion, sliced
1½ cups mushrooms, sliced
I cup frozen peas, thawed
⅓ cup frozen corn, thawed
4 eggs
⅔ cup milk
I tsp Cajun seasoning (optional)
2 tbsp chopped fresh parsley
salt (optional)

sunflower oil

potatoes

onion

mushrooms

peas

corn

eggs

Cajun seasoning

milk

fresh parsley

COOK'S TIP
Make sure the frying pan can safely be used under the broiler. Shield wooden handles with foil.

1 Heat the oil in a large frying pan and fry the potatoes and onion for 3–4 minutes, stirring often. Lower the heat, cover the pan and fry gently for 8–10 minutes more, until the potatoes are almost tender.

2 Add the mushrooms to the pan and cook for 2–3 minutes more, stirring often, until they have softened.

3 Add the peas and corn and stir them into the potato mixture.

4 Put the eggs and milk in a bowl. Add the Cajun seasoning and a little salt, if you like; beat well.

5 Level the top of the vegetables and scatter the parsley on top. Pour on the egg mixture and cook over a low heat for 10–15 minutes.

6 Put the pan under a hot broiler to set the top of the tortilla. Serve hot or cold, cut into wedges.

Three Bean Salad with Yogurt Dressing

This tangy bean and pasta salad is full of protein – and flavor – and is bound to be a favorite.

Serves 3–4

INGREDIENTS
¾ cup penne or other dried pasta
    shapes
2 tomatoes
7 oz can red kidney beans, drained
7 oz can cannellini beans, drained
7 oz can chickpeas, drained
1 green bell pepper, seeded and diced
3 tbsp plain yogurt
1 tbsp sunflower oil
grated rind of ½ lemon
1 tsp wholegrain mustard
1 tsp chopped fresh oregano
salt and ground black pepper

penne

tomatoes

red kidney beans

cannellini beans

chickpeas

green bell pepper

plain yogurt

sunflower oil

lemon

fresh oregano

wholegrain mustard

1 Bring a large pan of salted water to the boil. Add the pasta and cook for 10–12 minutes until just tender. Drain, cool under cold water and drain again.

2 Using a small, sharp knife, cut a cross in each of the tomatoes. Plunge them into a bowl of boiling water for 30 seconds. Remove with a slotted spoon or spatula, run under cold water and peel away the skins. Cut the tomatoes into segments.

3 Drain the canned beans and chickpeas in a colander, rinse them under cold water and drain again. Tip them into a bowl. Add the tomato segments, green pepper and pasta.

4 Whisk the yogurt until smooth. Gradually whisk in the oil, lemon rind and mustard. Stir in the oregano and add a little salt and pepper to taste. Pour the dressing over the salad and toss well.

Summer Pasta Salad

Tender young vegetables in a light dressing make a colourful and delicious lunch.

Serves 2–3

INGREDIENTS
2 cups fusilli or other dried
    pasta shapes
¹/₂ cup baby carrots, trimmed
    and halved
¹/₂ cup baby corn, halved lengthways
2oz snowpeas
4oz young asparagus spears, trimmed
4 scallions, trimmed and shredded
2 tsp white wine vinegar
4 tbsp extra virgin olive oil
1 tbsp wholegrain mustard
salt and ground black pepper

fusilli baby carrots baby corn

snowpeas asparagus spears

scallions white wine vinegar

olive oil wholegrain mustard

COOK'S TIP

Some children relish raw vegetables, but others prefer them cooked. Cut the cooking time slightly, and preserve the vitamins.

1 Bring a large pan of salted water to the boil. Add the pasta and cook for 10–12 minutes, until just tender. Meanwhile, cook the carrots and baby corn in a second pan of boiling salted water for 5 minutes.

2 Add the snowpeas and asparagus to the carrot mixture and cook for 2–3 minutes more. Drain all the vegetables and refresh under cold running water. Drain again.

3 Tip the vegetable mixture into a mixing bowl, add the spring onions and toss well together.

4 Drain the pasta, refresh it under cold running water and drain again. Toss with the vegetables. Mix the vinegar, olive oil and mustard in a jar. Add salt and pepper to taste, close the jar tightly and shake well. Pour the dressing over the salad. Mix and serve.

Cheese, Onion and Mushroom Flan

A tasty savory flan, ideal served with slices of wholemeal bread and a mixed leaf salad for extra fiber, vitamins and minerals.

COOK'S TIP
Make this savory flan in advance and freeze for up to 3 months. Thaw thoroughly and reheat to serve.

Serves 6

INGREDIENTS
1½ cups plain whole-wheat flour
pinch of salt
¾ stick butter or margarine
1 onion, sliced
1 leek, sliced
1½ cups mushrooms, chopped
2 tbsp vegetable stock
2 eggs
⅔ cup milk
1 cup frozen corn, thawed
2 tbsp snipped fresh chives
1 tbsp chopped fresh parsley
¾ cup finely grated Cheddar cheese
fresh chives, to garnish

whole-wheat flour
margarine
onion
eggs
leek
vegetable stock
mushrooms
fresh chives
corn
fresh parsley
grated Cheddar cheese

1 Sift the flour and salt into a bowl. Rub in the margarine or butter until the mixture resembles breadcrumbs and is not lumpy.

2 Add just enough cold water to form a soft dough. Knead lightly, wrap and chill for 30 minutes.

3 Put the onion, leek, mushrooms and vegetable stock into a pan. Cover and cook gently for 10 minutes, until the vegetables are just tender. Drain and set aside.

4 Preheat the oven to 400°F. Roll out the pastry on a lightly floured surface and use to line a 8in flan pan or dish. Trim the edges to neaten. Place the flan base on a baking sheet.

5 Spoon the vegetables over the flan base. Beat the eggs and milk together in a bowl, add the corn, herbs and cheese and mix well.

6 Pour the mixture over the vegetables. Bake for 20 minutes, then lower the oven temperature to 350°F, and cook for 30 minutes more, until set and lightly browned. Garnish with chives and serve warm or cold in slices.

Herb Omelette with Tomato Salad

This can be prepared in a few minutes. Use flavoursome, fresh plum tomatoes when in season. They are complemented by a tasty dressing.

Serves 4

INGREDIENTS
4 eggs, beaten
2 tbsp chopped, mixed fresh herbs,
    such as chives, marjoram, thyme or
    parsley, or 2 tsp dried mixed herbs
pat of butter
3 tbsp olive oil
1 tbsp fresh orange juice
1 tsp red wine vinegar
1 tsp wholegrain mustard
2 large beefsteak tomatoes, thinly sliced
salt and ground black pepper (optional)
fresh herb sprigs, to garnish

eggs

mixed fresh herbs

butter

olive oil

orange juice

red wine vinegar

wholegrain mustard

tomatoes

1 Beat the eggs and herbs in a bowl. Add a little salt and pepper, if you like. Heat the butter and a little of the oil in an omelette pan.

2 When the fats are just sizzling, pour in the egg mixture and leave to set, stirring very occasionally with a fork. This omelette needs to be almost cooked through (about 5 minutes).

3 Meanwhile, make a warm dressing by heating the rest of the oil with the orange juice, vinegar and mustard in a small pan over a low heat. When it is heated through, cover the pan and leave aside until needed.

COOK'S TIP
A great way to introduce children to herbs is to let them grow some. Brightly colored pots of chives, marjoram, thyme and parsley look good on a sunny window-sill and do not need a great deal of attention.

4 Roll up the cooked omelette and cut it neatly into ½in wide strips and transfer immediately to plates. Add the sliced tomatoes and pour on the warm dressing. Garnish with herb sprigs and serve at once.

Calzone

Pizza pasties filled with cheesy vegetables are perfect for picnics and packed lunches.

Makes 4

INGREDIENTS
4 cups all-purpose flour
pinch of salt
$^1/_4$ oz sachet rapid-rise dried yeast
$1^1/_2$ cups warm water
milk, to glaze
fresh herbs, to garnish

FOR THE FILLING
1 tbsp olive oil
1 medium red onion, thinly sliced
3 zucchini, total weight about
   12 oz, sliced
2 large tomatoes, diced
5oz mozzarella cheese, diced
1 tbsp chopped fresh oregano
salt and ground black pepper (optional)

flour   yeast   olive oil

red onion   zucchini   tomatoes

mozzarella cheese   fresh oregano

milk

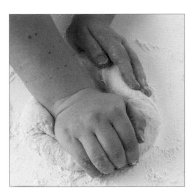

1 Sift the flour and salt into a bowl and sprinkle in the yeast. Stir in just enough warm water to mix to a soft dough. Knead for 5 minutes. Cover and leave in a warm place for about 1 hour, or until doubled in size.

2 Meanwhile, make the filling. Heat the oil and sauté the onion and zucchini for 3–4 minutes. Remove from the heat and add the tomatoes, cheese and oregano. Add a little salt and pepper, if you like.

3 Preheat the oven to 425°F. Knead the dough lightly and divide into four. Roll out each piece on a lightly floured surface to a 8in round and place a quarter of the filling on one half.

4 Brush the edges with milk and fold over to enclose the filling. Press the edges firmly to seal. Place on lightly oiled baking sheets, brush with milk, then make a small hole in each calzone to allow steam to escape. Bake for 15–20 minutes. Serve hot or cold.

Peanut Butter Fingers

Children cheer when these come on the scene. Make up a batch and freeze some ready for whenever there are young tummies to fill!

Makes 12

INGREDIENTS
2¼lb potatoes
3 tbsp sunflower oil
1 large onion, chopped
2 large red or green bell peppers,
    seeded and chopped
3 carrots, coarsely grated
2 zucchini, coarsely grated
1 cup mushrooms, chopped
1 tbsp dried mixed herbs
1 cup mature Cheddar cheese, grated
½ cup crunchy peanut butter
2 eggs, beaten
½ cup dried breadcrumbs
3 tbsp grated Parmesan cheese
oil, for deep frying
green salad, to serve

1 Halve the potatoes, if large. Bring to the boil in a pan of water, then simmer for 20 minutes, or until very tender. Mash thoroughly. Heat the oil in a large frying pan and fry the onion, peppers and carrots over a low heat for 5 minutes. Add the zucchini and mushrooms and cook for a further 5 minutes more.

2 Tip the mashed potato into a bowl and stir in the vegetable mixture, dried herbs, grated Cheddar cheese and peanut butter. Allow to cool for 30 minutes, then stir in half the beaten egg. Divide the mixture into 12 and shape into croquettes. Chill until firm.

potatoes
sunflower oil
onion
mushrooms
bell peppers
carrots
dried mixed herbs
grated Cheddar cheese
zucchini
dried breadcrumbs
eggs
Parmesan cheese
peanut butter

COOK'S TIP
If the potato mixture sticks to your fingers when you are shaping the croquettes, wash your hands well, then dip them in cold water before trying again.

3 Put the remaining beaten egg in a shallow bowl; mix the breadcrumbs and Parmesan cheese in another shallow bowl. Dip each croquette in turn in egg, then in the cheese mixture until evenly coated. Return to the fridge to set.

4 Heat oil in a deep fat frier to 375°F, then fry the croquettes in batches for about 3 minutes until golden. Drain well on kitchen paper. Serve hot with the green salad.

Bean Burgers

Although these are a bit fiddly, they are a delicious alternative to shop-bought burgers.

Serves 6

INGREDIENTS
1 cup long grain brown rice
2 tbsp sunflower oil
1/2 stick butter
1 onion, chopped
2 garlic cloves, crushed
1 small green bell pepper, seeded and chopped
1 carrot, coarsely grated
14oz can aduki beans, drained (or 4oz dried weight, soaked and cooked)
1 egg, beaten
1 cup Cheddar cheese, grated
1 tsp dried thyme
1/2 cup roasted hazelnuts
salt and ground black pepper
whole-wheat flour, for coating
oil, for frying
whole-wheat buns, salad and relish, to serve

brown rice
onion
garlic
sunflower oil
butter
green bell pepper
aduki beans
egg
carrot
hazelnuts
grated Cheddar cheese
dried thyme

1 Cook the rice in a large pan of boiling water for about 40 minutes until it is very soft and has absorbed most of the liquid. Drain the rice and transfer it to a large bowl.

2 Heat the oil and butter in a frying pan and fry the onion, garlic, green pepper and carrot for about 10 minutes until softened. Tip the mixture into the rice, together with the aduki beans, egg, cheese, thyme and nuts. Season lightly, then chill until quite firm.

3 Shape and divide the rice mixture into 12 patties, using wet hands if the mixture sticks. Coat the patties in whole-wheat flour and set aside.

4 Heat oil for shallow-frying in a large frying pan. Fry the burgers in batches until browned on each side, about 5 minutes in total. Remove and drain on kitchen paper. Serve in buns with salad and relish.

Vegetable Paella

Set this delicious dish down in front of your children and watch the paella vanish. It is surprising how much even reluctant eaters will get through when they are allowed to help themselves.

Serves 6

INGREDIENTS
1 onion, chopped
2 garlic cloves, crushed
2 leeks, sliced
3 celery sticks, chopped
1 red bell pepper, seeded and sliced
2 zucchini, sliced
2½ cups brown cap mushrooms, sliced
1½ cups frozen peas
2 cups long grain brown rice
14oz can cannellini beans, drained
3¾ cups vegetable stock
few saffron threads
2 cups cherry tomatoes
3–4 tbsp chopped fresh mixed herbs
lemon wedges and celery leaves,
     to garnish (optional)

onion
garlic
celery
courgettes zucchini
leeks
red bell pepper
brown cap mushrooms
peas
brown rice
vegetable stock
saffron threads
cannellini beans
cherry tomatoes
fresh mixed herbs

1 Put the onion, garlic, leeks, celery, pepper, zucchini and mushrooms in a large pan and mix together.

2 Add the peas, rice, cannellini beans, stock and saffron threads.

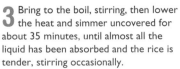

3 Bring to the boil, stirring, then lower the heat and simmer uncovered for about 35 minutes, until almost all the liquid has been absorbed and the rice is tender, stirring occasionally.

4 Halve the cherry tomatoes and stir them in together with the chopped herbs. Serve at once, garnished with lemon wedges and celery leaves.

Best-ever Bean Pot

After a game of soccer or an afternoon's walk in the woods, there's no nicer dish to come home to than this warming winter casserole.

COOK'S TIP
If you're short of time use canned navy beans – you'll need two 14oz cans. Drain, reserving the bean juices and make these up to 1⅔ cups with vegetable stock.

Serves 6

INGREDIENTS
2 cups dried navy beans
7½ cups water
1 bay leaf
2 onions
3 whole cloves
1 tsp olive oil
1–2 garlic cloves, crushed
2 leeks, thickly sliced
12 baby carrots
1 cup white mushrooms
14oz can chopped tomatoes
1 tbsp tomato paste
1 tbsp chopped fresh thyme
2 tbsp chopped fresh parsley
2 cups fresh white breadcrumbs
salt and ground black pepper
French bread, to serve

bay leaf

cloves

navy beans

onions

garlic

olive oil

baby carrots

mushrooms

leeks

chopped tomatoes

tomato paste

breadcrumbs

fresh parsley

fresh thyme

1 Soak the beans overnight in plenty of cold water. Drain and rinse under cold running water. Put them in a pan and add the water and the bay leaf. Bring to the boil and cook rapidly for 10 minutes.

2 Peel one of the onions and spike it with cloves. Add to the beans and lower the heat. Cover and simmer for 1 hour, until the beans are almost tender. Drain, reserving the stock but discarding the bay leaf and spiked onion.

3 Chop the remaining onion. Heat the oil in a large flameproof casserole and fry the onion with the garlic over a low heat for 5 minutes, or until softened.

4 Preheat the oven to 325°F. Add the leeks, carrots, mushrooms, chopped tomatoes, tomato purée, thyme to the casserole. Stir in 1⅔ cups of the reserved stock.

5 Bring to the boil, cover and simmer gently for 10 minutes. Stir in the cooked beans and parsley. Season lightly.

6 Sprinkle with the breadcrumbs. Bake, uncovered, for 35 minutes, or until the topping is golden brown and crisp. Serve hot, with chunks of bread, if you like.

Popeye's Pie

Children who spurn spinach will change their tune when invited to try this tasty filo pie.

Serves 4

INGREDIENTS
3/4 stick butter
1 tsp grated nutmeg
2lb fresh spinach leaves, washed and
   large stalks removed
2/3 cup feta cheese, crumbled
1/2 cup grated Cheddar cheese
10oz filo pastry, thawed if frozen
1 tsp pumpkin pie spice

grated
nutmeg

butter

feta cheese

spinach

grated
Cheddar
cheese

pumpkin pie spice

filo pastry

COOK'S TIP

Work with one sheet of filo at a time, keeping the rest covered with a damp tea towel as they dry out very quickly and become brittle.

1 Melt 1/4 stick butter in a large frying pan and add the nutmeg and the spinach. Cover the pan and cook for 5 minutes, or until the spinach is tender. Drain well, pressing out as much liquid as possible.

2 Preheat the oven to 325°F. Melt the remaining butter in a small pan. Mix the cheeses together in a bowl. Grease a small, deep baking tin with melted butter and fit a sheet of filo into the base. Brush the filo with melted butter.

3 Continue to lay pastry sheets across the base and up the sides of the tin, brushing each time with butter, until two-thirds of the pastry has been used. Don't worry if the filo flops over the top – this will be tidied up later.

4 Mix the grated cheeses and spinach and spread the mixture into the tin. Fold the edges of the filo over. Crumple the remaining sheets of filo and arrange them over the top of the filling. Brush with melted butter and sprinkle with the mixed spice. Bake for 45 minutes, then increase the oven temperature to 400°F for 10–15 minutes more. Garnish with cherry tomatoes.

Aubergine Bolognese

This excellent pasta sauce combines a variety of tasty vegetables with lentils.

Serves 4–6

INGREDIENTS
1 tbsp sunflower oil
4oz eggplant, diced
½ red bell pepper, seeded and diced
½ yellow or orange bell pepper,
    seeded and diced
1 leek, sliced
1 large carrot, diced
1 garlic clove, crushed
½ cup frozen corn
½ cup red lentils
14oz can chopped tomatoes
2 cups vegetable stock
pinch of dried herbs
1 cup dried pasta shapes
pat of butter
½ cup grated Cheddar cheese
salt and ground black pepper

1 Heat the oil in a medium pan, add the vegetables and fry over a gentle heat for 3 minutes, stirring frequently, until they have softened slightly.

sunflower oil

eggplant

bell peppers

garlic

carrot

corn

leek

dried mixed herbs

pasta shapes

red lentils

chopped tomatoes

vegetable stock

butter

grated Cheddar cheese

COOK'S TIP
For extra flavor, stir a little yeast extract into the Bolognese. It goes very well with eggplants and lentils.

2 Add the garlic, corn, lentils, tomatoes, stock, herbs and a little salt and pepper. Bring to the boil, lower the heat, cover and simmer for about 30 minutes, stirring occasionally and adding a little extra stock if necessary.

3 About 10 minutes before the vegetable and lentil mixture is ready, bring a pan of water to the boil and cook the pasta for 10 minutes until tender. Drain, toss in a little butter, then spoon on to plates. Top with the eggplant Bolognese, sprinkle with the cheese and serve.

Ratatouille Rumbletum

Marinating tofu in soya sauce gives it a wonderful flavor. It makes a very good addition to this hearty vegetable and pasta dish.

Serves 6

INGREDIENTS
1 small eggplant, cubed
2 zucchini, sliced
7oz firm tofu, cubed
2 tbsp dark soy sauce
3 garlic cloves, crushed
2 tsp sesame seeds
2 tbsp olive oil
1 small red bell pepper, seeded and sliced
1 onion, finely chopped
$\frac{2}{3}$ cup vegetable stock
3 firm ripe tomatoes, skinned, seeded and quartered
1 tbsp chopped mixed fresh herbs
2 cups penne
salt
crusty bread, to serve

soy sauce

garlic

sesame seeds

tofu

olive oil

onion

red bell pepper

vegetable stock

tomatoes

penne

fresh mixed herbs

1 Place the eggplant and zucchini in a colander. Sprinkle with salt and leave to drain for 30 minutes, then rinse well and pat dry.

2 Mix the tofu with the soy sauce, a third of the crushed garlic and all the sesame seeds. Cover and marinate for 30 minutes. Meanwhile, sauté the eggplant and zucchini in the olive oil until lightly browned.

3 Put the pepper, onion and remaining garlic into a pan with the stock. Bring to the boil, cover and cook for 5 minutes, until the vegetables are tender. Remove the lid and boil until all the stock has evaporated. Add the tomatoes and herbs. Cook for 3 minutes more.

4 Cook the pasta in a large pan of boiling water for 10–12 minutes until just tender. Drain thoroughly and toss with all the vegetables and tofu. Transfer to a shallow 10in ovenproof dish and broil until lightly toasted. Serve with crusty bread.

Macaroni Cheese with Mushrooms

Here's an upmarket version of an all-time classic, with mushrooms and pine nuts.

Serves 4

INGREDIENTS
4 cups quick-cooking
    elbow macaroni
3 tbsp olive oil
2 cups white mushrooms, sliced
2 fresh thyme sprigs
$\frac{1}{4}$ cup all-purpose flour
1 vegetable stock cube
$2\frac{1}{2}$ cups milk
$\frac{1}{2}$ tsp celery salt
$1\frac{1}{2}$ cups grated Cheddar cheese
1 tsp Dijon mustard (optional)
$\frac{1}{3}$ cup freshly grated Parmesan cheese
$\frac{1}{3}$ cup pine nuts

1 Bring a pan of salted water to the boil. Add the macaroni and cook for about 8 minutes or until tender.

macaroni

olive oil

white mushrooms

fresh thyme

vegetable stock cube

milk

flour

celery salt

grated Cheddar cheese

Parmesan cheese

pine nuts

COOK'S TIP
It used to be difficult to locate vegetarian cheeses, but stores now carry quite a wide range, made without rennet from animal sources.

2 Heat the oil in a heavy pan. Add the mushrooms and thyme, cover and cook over a gentle heat for 2–3 minutes. Stir in the flour, crumble in the stock cube and stir continuously until evenly blended. Pour in the milk a little at a time, stirring after each addition. Add the celery salt and Cheddar cheese. Stir in the mustard, if using, then simmer the sauce briefly for 1–2 minutes until thickened.

3 Preheat the broiler. Drain the macaroni well, toss into the sauce and divide among four individual gratin dishes or pour into one large gratin dish. Scatter with the grated Parmesan cheese and pine nuts, then grill until brown and bubbly.

Vegetarian Lasagne

Ready-to-use lasagne is a real boon to the busy parent. It means preparing a delicious dish like this is (almost) child's play.

COOK'S TIP
Leave the lasagne to stand for 10 minutes before serving. It will firm up slightly and will be easier to slice.

Serves 6–8

INGREDIENTS
1 small eggplant
1 large onion, finely chopped
2 garlic cloves, crushed
1¼ cups vegetable stock
2 cups mushrooms, sliced
14oz can chopped tomatoes
2 tbsp tomato paste
¼ tsp ground fresh root ginger
1 tsp mixed dried herbs
10–12 sheets ready-to-use lasagne
scant 1 cup cottage cheese
1 egg, beaten
2 tbsp freshly grated Parmesan cheese
¼ cup grated Cheddar cheese

FOR THE SAUCE
¼ stick butter or margarine
¼ cup all-purpose flour
1¼ cups milk
large pinch of grated nutmeg
salt and ground black pepper

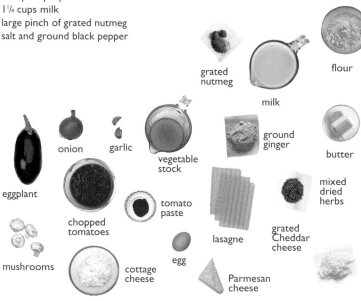

grated nutmeg
milk
flour
ground ginger
butter
vegetable stock
mixed dried herbs
onion
garlic
eggplant
tomato paste
chopped tomatoes
lasagne
grated Cheddar cheese
mushrooms
egg
cottage cheese
Parmesan cheese

1 Cut the aubergine into 1in cubes. Sprinkle with salt, leave for about 30 minutes and rinse. Put the onion and garlic into a pan with the stock. Bring to the boil, lower the heat, cover and cook for 10 minutes.

2 Add the diced eggplant, sliced mushrooms, tomatoes, tomato purée, ginger and herbs. Bring to the boil, cover and cook for 15–20 minutes. Remove the lid and cook rapidly to evaporate the liquid by half.

3 Make the sauce. Put the butter, flour, milk and nutmeg into a pan. Whisk together over the heat until thickened and smooth. Season to taste.

4 Preheat the oven to 400°F. Spoon about a third of the vegetable mixture into the base of a 12 x 8 x 2in ovenproof dish. Cover with a layer of lasagne and a quarter of the white sauce.

5 Repeat to make two more layers, then cover with the cottage cheese. Beat the egg into the remaining white sauce and pour it over the top. Sprinkle with the grated Parmesan and Cheddar. Bake for 25–30 minutes or until the top is golden brown.

Stuffed Vegetables

Peppers, eggplant and tomatoes all make colorful containers for savory fillings. Serve a selection with thick, creamy yogurt.

Serves 6

INGREDIENTS
1 medium eggplant
1 large green bell pepper
2 large tomatoes
3 tbsp olive oil, plus extra,
    for sprinkling
1 large onion, chopped
2 garlic cloves, crushed
1 cup long grain brown rice
2½ cups vegetable stock
1 cup pine nuts
⅓ cup currants
3 tbsp chopped fresh dill
3 tbsp chopped fresh parsley
1 tbsp chopped fresh mint
salt
fresh dill sprigs, to garnish
natural strained plain yogurt, to serve

eggplant   bell pepper   tomatoes

garlic   olive oil

onion   brown rice

fresh mint   currants   fresh parsley

pine nuts   fresh dill   vegetable stock

1 Halve the eggplant, scoop out the flesh with a sharp knife and chop finely. Salt the inside of each aubergine shell and drain upside down for 20 minutes so that they will not be too spongy once cooked. Meanwhile, cut the pepper in half and remove the core and seeds. Cut the tops from the tomatoes, scoop out the insides and chop roughly, with the tomato tops.

2 Heat the oil in a frying pan. Add the onion, garlic and chopped eggplant and fry for 10 minutes, then stir in the rice and cook for 2 minutes. Add the tomato flesh, stock, pine nuts and currants. Bring to the boil, cover, then simmer for 15 minutes.

3 Blanch the eggplant and green pepper halves in a pan of boiling water for about 3 minutes, then drain them upside down.

4 Preheat the oven to 375°F. Stir the herbs into the rice filling then spoon it into all six vegetable containers. Place in a lightly greased baking dish, drizzle some olive oil over and bake for 25–30 minutes. Serve hot, topped with yogurt and dill sprigs.

Shepherdess Pie

This tasty dish also excludes milk, butter and cheese, so is suitable for vegans or children who cannot tolerate dairy products.

Serves 6–8

INGREDIENTS
2¼ lb potatoes
3 tbsp extra virgin olive oil
3 tbsp sunflower oil
1 large onion, chopped
1 green bell pepper, seeded and
    chopped
2 carrots, coarsely grated
2 garlic cloves
1 cup mushrooms, chopped
2 x 14oz cans aduki beans, drained
2½ cups vegetable stock
1 tsp vegetable yeast extract
2 bay leaves
1 tsp dried mixed herbs
dried breadcrumbs or chopped nuts,
    for sprinkling
salt and ground black pepper

potatoes   olive oil   sunflower
                         oil

onion   green bell   carrots
         pepper

garlic   mushrooms   aduki
                       beans

vegetable   yeast   bay leaves   breadcrumbs   dried
stock   extract   mixed
                                                  herbs

1 Scrub the potatoes, then boil them in their skins until tender. Drain, reserving a little of the cooking water to moisten them.

2 Mash the potatoes well, mixing in the olive oil until you have a smooth purée. Season lightly.

3 Heat the sunflower oil in a frying pan. Add the onion and pepper and fry for 2 minutes, then add the carrots and garlic and cook for 5 minutes more, until soft. Stir in the mushrooms and beans, cook for 2 minutes, then add the stock, yeast extract, bay leaves and mixed herbs. Simmer for 15 minutes.

4 Remove the bay leaves and tip the vegetable mixture into a shallow baking dish. Spoon on the potatoes in dollops and sprinkle with the crumbs or nuts. Broil until golden brown. Serve hot.

Star Vegetable Pie

How do you persuade children to eat turnips and rutabaga? Make them part of a tasty vegetable medley and top them with a galaxy of stars.

Serves 4–6

INGREDIENTS
3 tbsp sunflower oil
1 onion, sliced
2 carrots, chopped
3 medium turnips, chopped
1 small rutabaga, chopped
2 celery sticks, thinly sliced
1/2 tsp dried mixed herbs
14oz can chopped tomatoes
14oz can chickpeas
1 vegetable stock cube
salt and ground black pepper

FOR THE TOPPING
2 cups self-rising flour
1 tsp baking powder
1/2 stick margarine
3 tbsp sunflower seeds
2 tbsp grated Parmesan cheese
2/3 cup milk, plus extra for glazing

1 Heat the oil in a pan and fry all the vegetables for about 10 minutes, until they are soft. Add the herbs, tomatoes, chickpeas (with the can liquid) and crumble the stock cube into the pan. Season lightly and simmer for about 20 minutes. Pour the mixture into a shallow casserole. Preheat the oven to 375°F.

sunflower oil

onion

carrots

celery

turnips

vegetable stock cube

dried mixed herbs

rutabaga

margarine

chickpeas

sunflower seeds

chopped tomatoes

self-rising flour

Parmesan cheese

milk

baking powder

2 Mix the flour and baking powder in a bowl. Rub in the margarine until it resembles crumbs. Stir in the seeds and Parmesan cheese. Add the milk, mix to a firm dough and roll out on a floured surface to a thickness of 1/2in. Stamp out stars or cut other shapes.

3 Place the shapes on top of the vegetable mixture and brush with a little extra milk. Bake for 12–15 minutes until risen and golden brown. Serve hot.

Veggie Tofu Stir-fry

High protein tofu tastes best when marinated lightly before cooking. If you use smoked tofu, the results will be even tastier.

Serves 4

INGREDIENTS
2 x 8oz cartons smoked
    tofu, cubed
3 tbsp soy sauce
2 tbsp grape juice
1 tbsp sesame oil
3 tbsp sunflower oil
2 leeks, thinly sliced
2 carrots, cut in sticks
1 large zucchini, thinly sliced
$\frac{2}{3}$ cup baby corn, halved
1 cup white or shiitake
    mushrooms, sliced
1 tbsp sesame seeds
cooked egg noodles, to serve

1 Marinate the tofu in the soy sauce, grape juice and sesame oil for at least 30 minutes. Drain and reserve the marinade for later.

smoked tofu — soy sauce — grape juice — sunflower oil — sesame oil — zucchini — baby corn — leeks — carrots — sesame seeds — egg noodles — mushrooms

VARIATION
Tofu is also excellent marinated and skewered, then lightly grilled. Push the tofu off the skewers into pockets of pitta bread. Fill with salad and serve with a dollop of strained plain yogurt. Alternatively, make skewers with tofu and vegetable pieces and serve as kebabs.

COOK'S TIP
If you don't have a wok, a deep frying pan or sauté pan is just as good.

2 Heat the sunflower oil in a wok and stir-fry the smoked tofu cubes until browned all over. Remove and reserve.

3 Add the leeks, carrots, zucchini and baby corn to the wok, stirring and tossing for about 2 minutes. Add the mushrooms and cook for 1 minute more. Return the tofu to the wok and pour in the marinade. Heat until bubbling, then scatter with the sesame seeds and serve with the hot noodles.

Party Pizza

Perfect for sharing, this tasty wholewheat
pizza can be served hot or cold.

Serves 6

INGREDIENTS
2 cups plain whole-wheat flour
pinch of salt
2 tsp baking powder
1/2 stick margarine
2/3 cup milk
2 tbsp tomato paste
2 tsp dried mixed herbs
1 tbsp olive oil
1 onion, sliced
1 garlic clove, crushed
2 small zucchini, sliced
1 cup mushrooms, sliced
2/3 cup frozen corn
2 plum tomatoes, sliced
1/2 cup grated Red Leicester cheese
1/2 cup grated mozzarella cheese
fresh basil sprigs, to garnish

whole-wheat flour · baking powder · margarine · milk · tomato paste · dried mixed herbs · olive oil · onion · garlic · zucchini · plum tomatoes · mushrooms · corn · grated Red Leicester cheese · mozzarella cheese · fresh basil

1 Preheat the oven to 425°F. Line a baking sheet with some baking parchment. Put the flour, salt and baking powder in a bowl and rub in the margarine until the mixture resembles breadcrumbs.

2 Add enough milk to form a soft dough and knead lightly. On a lightly floured surface, roll out the dough to a circle about 10in in diameter.

3 Place the dough on the prepared baking sheet and pinch up the edges to make a rim. Spread the tomato paste on the base and sprinkle over the herbs.

4 Heat the oil in a frying pan, add the onion, garlic, zucchini and mushrooms and cook gently for 10 minutes, stirring from time to time.

5 Spread the fried vegetables over the pizza base and sprinkle the corn over. Arrange the tomato slices in a layer on top.

VARIATION
The vegetable mixture can be varied. Red, orange or yellow bell peppers make a good addition, while celery contributes crunch.

6 Mix together the cheeses and sprinkle over the pizza. Bake for 25–30 minutes, until cooked and golden brown. Serve the pizza hot or cold in slices, garnished with the basil sprigs.

COOK'S TIP
This pizza is ideal for freezing in portions or slices. Freeze for up to 3 months.

Pumpkin and Pistachio Risotto

Treat your vegetarian teenagers to this elegant combination of creamy golden rice and orange pumpkin. The flavor is superb.

Serves 4

INGREDIENTS
5 cups vegetable stock
generous pinch of saffron threads
2 tbsp olive oil
1 onion, chopped
2 garlic cloves, crushed
2 cups arborio risotto rice
2lb pumpkin, peeled, seeded and cut into ³/₄in cubes
²/₃ cup unsweetened apple juice
2 tbsp finely grated Parmesan cheese
¹/₂ cup pistachio nuts
3 tbsp chopped fresh marjoram or oregano, plus extra leaves, to garnish
salt, grated nutmeg and ground black pepper, to serve

1 Bring the stock to the boil in a an and reduce to a simmer. Ladle a little stock into a small bowl. Add the saffron threads and leave to infuse.

2 Heat the oil in a large pan. Add the onion and garlic and cook gently for about 5 minutes. Add the rice and pumpkin and cook for a few more minutes until the rice looks transparent.

3 Pour in the apple juice and allow it to bubble hard. When it is absorbed add a quarter of the stock and the infused saffron and liquid. Stir constantly until all the liquid has been absorbed.

vegetable stock

saffron

olive oil

onion

garlic

Parmesan cheese

apple juice

pumpkin

arborio risotto rice

pistachio nuts

fresh marjoram

4 Gradually add hot stock, a ladleful at a time, allowing the rice to absorb the liquid before adding more, and stirring all the time. After 20–30 minutes the rice should be golden yellow and creamy. When tested, the grains should be tender, but retain a bit of bite.

5 Stir in the Parmesan cheese, cover the pan and leave to stand for 5 minutes. To finish, stir in the pistachios and marjoram or oregano. Season to taste with a little salt, nutmeg and pepper, and sprinkle over a few extra marjoram or oregano leaves.

Side Dishes

Roasted Vegetables

Don't stick to roast spuds! A good roasting brings out the colors and flavors of other vegetables too.

Serves 4

INGREDIENTS

1 eggplant, cut in large chunks
1 red bell pepper, seeded and cut in thick strips
1 green bell pepper, seeded and cut in thick strips
1 yellow bell pepper, seeded and cut in thick strips
1 zucchini, cut in large chunks
1 onion, cut in thick slices
1 cup small mushrooms
8oz plum tomatoes, quartered
5 tbsp olive oil
4–5 fresh thyme sprigs
2 fresh oregano sprigs
3–4 fresh rosemary sprigs
salt and ground black pepper

eggplant

bell peppers

zucchini

onion

mushrooms

plum tomatoes

olive oil

fresh thyme

fresh oregano

fresh rosemary

1 Arrange the eggplant chunks on a plate and sprinkle them with salt. Leave for 30 minutes.

2 Squeeze the eggplant to remove as much liquid as possible. Rinse off the salt. This process stops the eggplant tasting bitter.

3 Preheat the oven to 400°F. Arrange all the vegetables, including the eggplant, in a roasting pan and drizzle with the oil.

4 Scatter most of the herb sprigs among the vegetables in the roasting pan and season lightly. Roast the vegetables for 20–25 minutes.

5 Turn the vegetables over and roast them for 15 minutes more, or until they are tender and browned.

6 Scatter the remaining fresh herb sprigs over the cooked vegetables just before serving.

COOK'S TIP

Try these flavor-packed vegetables as a filling for pitta pockets, stuffed with spoonfuls of hummus.

Sizzling Tomatoes

Many children love garlic, especially if they're used to it, but if yours aren't keen, simply leave it out or substitute chopped fresh parsley.

Serves 4

INGREDIENTS
3 tbsp butter, softened
1 large garlic clove, crushed
1 tsp finely grated orange rind
4 firm plum tomatoes, or 2 large
    beefsteak tomatoes
salt and ground black pepper
fresh basil leaves, to garnish

butter   garlic   orange rind

tomatoes   fresh basil

1 Preheat the oven to 400°F. Cream the butter in a bowl. Mix in the crushed garlic, orange rind, and a little salt and pepper. Chill in the refrigerator for a few minutes.

2 Halve the tomatoes crossways, trim the bases and stand them in a baking dish. Spread the butter over the tomatoes and bake for 15–25 minutes, until just tender. Serve garnished with the basil.

Carrot Salad

Raw carrots can be a little bland. Give them a lift with a lemony dressing and they'll be transformed into a zesty side dish.

Serves 4–6

INGREDIENTS
1lb small, young carrots
grated rind and juice of ½ lemon
1 tbsp soft light brown sugar
4 tbsp sunflower oil
1 tsp sesame oil
1 tsp chopped fresh oregano, plus
    oregano sprigs, to garnish

carrots   lemon   brown sugar

sunflower oil   sesame oil   fresh oregano

1 Finely grate the carrots and place them in a large bowl. Stir in the lemon rind, 1–2 tbsp of the lemon juice, the sugar and both oils. Mix well.

2 Taste and add more lemon juice, if needed. Sprinkle the oregano on top, toss lightly and cover. Leave the salad for 1 hour before serving, garnished with the oregano.

Confetti Salad

This appetizing and colorful rice salad is ideal for a healthy and tasty packed lunch.

Serves 4–6

INGREDIENTS
1 cup mixed brown and wild rice
1 yellow bell pepper, seeded
   and diced
1 bunch scallions, chopped
3 celery sticks, chopped
1 large beefsteak tomato, chopped
2 green eating apples, chopped
3/4 cup ready-to-eat dried
   apricots, chopped
2/3 cup raisins
4 tbsp unsweetened apple juice
2 tbsp light soy sauce
2 tbsp chopped fresh parsley
1 tbsp chopped fresh rosemary
salt and ground black pepper

mixed brown and wild rice

yellow bell pepper

scallions

beefsteak tomato

eating apples

celery

dried apricots

raisins

unsweetened apple juice

soy sauce

fresh parsley

fresh rosemary

1 Cook the rice in a large pan of boiling water for about 30 minutes or until just tender. Tip the rice into a colander, rinse under cold running water to cool quickly and drain thoroughly.

2 Place the pepper, spring onions, celery, tomato, apples, apricots, raisins and cooked rice in a serving bowl and mix well.

COOK'S TIP
If you have time, chop the vegetables very finely. Small children often cope with them better that way.

3 In a small bowl, mix together the apple juice, soy sauce and herbs. Add a little salt and pepper and mix together well.

4 Pour the dressing over the rice mixture and toss the ingredients together to mix. Serve immediately or cover and chill in the refrigerator before serving.

Mighty Mash

These creamy mashed potatoes are perfect with vegetable bakes – and although there seems to be a lot of garlic, the flavor is sweet and subtle when cooked in this way.

Serves 6–8

INGREDIENTS
2 garlic bulbs, separated into cloves
    but not peeled
1 stick butter
3lb baking potatoes, peeled
    and quartered
$\frac{1}{2}$ cup milk
salt

garlic

butter

milk

baking
potatoes

COOK'S TIP
When cooking the blanched garlic cloves, keep the heat low and shake the pan frequently to prevent the garlic from scorching.

1 Blanch the garlic cloves in boiling water for 2 minutes, then drain and peel. Melt half the butter in a frying pan. Add the blanched garlic cloves, cover and cook gently for 20–25 minutes until very tender and just golden.

2 Tip the contents of the pan into a blender or a food processor and process until smooth. Scrape into a small bowl, press plastic wrap on to the surface to prevent a skin from forming and set aside.

3 Put the potatoes in a large pan of cold water. Bring to the boil and cook for 30 minutes or until very tender. Drain, then return to the pan. Mash thoroughly.

4 Heat the milk until just below boiling point, then gradually beat it into the potatoes, with the remaining butter and reserved garlic purée. Season lightly with salt, if needed.

Speedy Mushrooms

To change this recipe into a light meal, serve these tasty mushrooms on whole-wheat toast or bagels. Leave out the garlic if the children don't like it. This is best served when it is very hot.

Serves 6

INGREDIENTS
6 cups mushrooms
6 tbsp olive oil
2 garlic cloves, finely chopped
   (optional)
3 tbsp finely chopped fresh parsley
salt and ground black pepper

mushrooms

garlic

fresh
parsley

olive oil

1 Clean the mushrooms carefully by wiping them with a damp cloth or kitchen paper. Take care not to let them get too wet.

2 Using a small sharp knife, cut off the woody tips of the stems and discard. Slice the stems and caps fairly thickly.

3 Heat the oil in a large frying pan. Stir in the garlic, if using, and mushrooms. Cook for 8–10 minutes, stirring occasionally. Season with salt and pepper to taste.

4 Stir in the parsley. Cook for about 5 minutes more, and serve at once, whilst piping hot.

COOK'S TIP

If you prefer not to fry the mushrooms in oil, try sweating them in vegetable stock instead. Put them in a pan with about 6 tbsp stock and cook until almost all the stock has been absorbed. Sprinkle a little soy sauce over them and serve.

Fruity Coleslaw

There's something about coleslaw that really appeals to kids. Whether it's the bright colors or the creamy dressing, the fact is that this is a great way of persuading them to eat fresh, raw vegetables.

Serves 4–6

INGREDIENTS
1lb white cabbage
1 medium Bermuda onion
2 apples
2 carrots, peeled
$^2/_3$ cup mayonnaise
1 tsp celery salt
fresh flat-leaf parsley, to garnish

white cabbage

onion

apples

carrots

mayonnaise

fresh parsley

celery salt

1 Discard any tough or discolored leaves from the outside of the cabbage, cut it into 2in wedges, then remove the stem section.

2 Peel the onion and cut into medium-sized slices. Roughly grate the carrots.

VARIATION

This recipe can be adapted easily to suit different tastes. For added texture, stir in 1 cup chopped walnuts or $^2/_3$ cup raisins. For a richer coleslaw, add ½ cup grated Cheddar cheese and serve it as a main dish.

3 Slice the cabbage by hand, or in a food processor fitted with a slicing blade. Peel and core the apples; reserve a few slices for a garnish, then grate the remaining apples finely.

4 Mix all the vegetables and apples in a large bowl. Fold in the mayonnaise, toss well and season with a little celery salt. Garnish with the reserved apple slices and flat-leaf parsley.

Potato Salad with Egg and Lemon Dressing

Potato salads are always popular. This one adds protein in the form of a hard-boiled egg.

Serves 4

INGREDIENTS

2lb salad or new potatoes
1 onion, finely chopped
1 egg, hard-boiled
1¼ cups mayonnaise
1 clove garlic, crushed (optional)
finely grated rind and juice of
    1 lemon
4tbsp chopped fresh parsley, plus a
    sprig of flat-leaf parsley, to garnish

potatoes

onion

mayonnaise

lemon

fresh
parsley

hard-boiled
egg

1 Peel the potatoes and rinse well. Place them in a pan of salted water and bring to the boil. Simmer for 20 minutes. Drain and allow to cool.

2 Cut the potatoes into large dice and mix with the onion in a bowl.

COOK'S TIP

Look out for salad potatoes in food stores. Varieties like Charlotte and Linzer Delikatess are ideal as they are full of flavor and hold their shape when boiled.

3 Shell the hard-boiled egg and grate it into a mixing bowl, then add the mayonnaise. Combine the garlic, if using, with the lemon rind and juice; stir into the mayonnaise.

4 Fold in the chopped parsley. Add the egg and lemon dressing to the potatoes, toss to coat and transfer to a salad bowl. Garnish with flat-leaf parsley and serve.

Desserts and Drinks

Tropical Treat

Food stores are full of wonderful fruits that make a really tangy salad when mixed together. Serve with cream or yogurt.

Serves 4

INGREDIENTS
1 small pineapple
2 Chinese gooseberry
1 ripe mango
1 watermelon slice
2 peaches
2 bananas
4 tbsp tropical fruit juice

pineapple

Chinese goosberry

mango

watermelon

peaches

bananas

tropical fruit juice

COOK'S TIP

For a children's party, serve the salad in a watermelon shell. Cut a medium watermelon in half, zig-zagging the knife to make a decorative edge. Make balls from the watermelon flesh and add to the salad.

1 Cut the pineapple into ½in slices. Work round the edge of each slice, cutting off the skin and any spiky bits. Cut each slice into wedges and put them in a bowl.

2 Peel the Chinese gooseberry, cut them in half lengthways and then into wedges. Add to the pineapple in the bowl.

3 Cut the mango lengthways into quarters cutting around the large flat pit. Peel the flesh and cut it into chunks or slices.

4 Cut the watermelon into slices, cut off the skin and cut the flesh into chunks. Remove the seeds. Cut the peaches in half, remove the pits and cut the flesh into wedges. Slice the bananas. Add all the fruit to the bowl and gently stir in the fruit juice.

Lazy Pastry Pudding

You don't need to be neat to make this dessert as it looks best when it's really craggy and rough. Serve with whipped cream or custard.

Serves 6

INGREDIENTS
2 cups all-purpose flour
1 tbsp superfine sugar
1 tbsp ground pumpkin pie spice
1 1/3 stick butter or margarine
1 egg, separated
1lb cooking apples
2 tbsp lemon juice
1/2 cup raw sugar
2/3 cup raisins
1/4 cup hazelnuts, toasted and chopped
custard, to serve (optional)

flour   superfine   pumpkin
              sugar   pie spice

                  egg

butter   apples

lemon

     raisins   raw sugar

        hazelnuts

Cook's Tip

When baking the pudding, cover the central hole in the pastry lid with foil, to stop the raisins from burning.

1 Mix the flour, sugar and spice in a bowl. Rub in the butter or margarine until the mixture resembles crumbs. Add the egg yolk and make a firm pastry. Add a little water if needed.

2 Knead the dough on a lightly floured surface until smooth, then roll to a rough circle, about 12in across. Use the rolling pin to lift the pastry on to a small baking sheet. The pastry should hang over the edges.

3 Peel and slice the apples. Toss them in the lemon juice. Sprinkle some of them over the middle of the pastry, leaving a 4in border all round. Reserve 2 tbsp of the raw sugar. Sprinkle some of the raisins over the top, then some of the remaining raw sugar. Keep making layers of apple, raisins and sugar until you have used them up.

4 Preheat the oven to 400°F. Fold up the pastry edges to cover the fruit, overlapping it where necessary. Don't worry too much about neatness. Brush the pastry with the egg white and sprinkle with the reserved raw sugar. Sprinkle the nuts over the top. Cook for 30–35 minutes, until the pastry is cooked and browned. Serve with custard, if you like.

Creamy Rice Pudding

Rice pudding is popular with children the world over.
The added egg yolks add to the rich, creamy texture.

Serves 4

INGREDIENTS
1/2 cup raisins
1/2 cup short grain rice
1 in strip of pared lime or lemon rind
1 cup water
2 cups full-fat whole milk
1 cup sugar
1 in cinnamon stick
2 egg yolks, well beaten
1 tbsp butter, cubed
toasted flaked almonds, to decorate
segments of fresh peeled oranges,
    to serve

short
grain
rice

raisins

lemon

milk

cinnamon
stick

sugar

egg yolks

butter

1 Put the raisins into a small bowl.
Pour over warm water to cover and
set aside to soak.

2 Put the short grain rice into a pan with the citrus rind and water. Bring slowly
to the boil, then lower the heat, cover and simmer very gently for 20 minutes
or until all the water has been absorbed.

3 Remove the citrus rind from the
rice and discard it. Add the milk,
sugar and cinnamon stick. Cook,
stirring, over a very low heat until all
the milk has been absorbed. Do not
cover the pan.

VARIATION
Use soft light brown sugar for added
flavor; this will team perfectly with
the raisins.

4 Remove and discard the cinnamon
stick. Add the egg yolks and cubed
butter to the rice, stirring constantly
until the butter has melted and the
pudding is rich and creamy. Drain the
raisins well and then stir them into the
rice. Cook the pudding for a few
minutes longer.

5 Transfer the rice into a dish and
cool. Decorate with the almonds
and serve with the orange segments.

COOK'S TIP
It is essential to use whole milk and
short grain rice for this pudding. Short
grain is sometimes packaged with the
name pudding rice.

Pancake Flips

Pancakes have loads of uses so make a double batch and freeze them between sheets of baking parchment for another day. The fruit and ice cream here make a delicious combination.

Serves 3

INGREDIENTS
½ cup all-purpose flour
I egg
⅔ cup milk
I tbsp sunflower oil

FOR THE FILLING
I banana
I orange
2–3 scoops ice cream
a little maple syrup

flour
egg
milk
sunflower oil
banana
orange
ice cream
maple syrup

1 Sift the flour into a bowl, add the egg and gradually whisk in the milk to form a smooth batter. Whisk in I tsp of the sunflower oil.

2 To make the filling, slice the banana thinly or cut it into chunks. Cut the peel away from the orange with a serrated knife, then cut the orange into segments.

3 Heat a little of the remaining oil in a non-stick frying pan, pour off any excess oil and add 2 tbsp of the batter. Tilt the pan to evenly coat the base and cook the batter for a couple of minutes until the pancake is set and the underside is golden.

4 Turn or toss the pancake, then brown the other side. Slide it on to a plate, fold in four and keep warm, while you make five more pancakes in the same way. Spoon a little fruit into each pancake and arrange on serving plates. Top with the remaining fruit, and add a scoop of ice cream and a little maple syrup. Serve.

COOK'S TIP

For the best results, allow your batter to stand for about an hour, and whisk again just before using. Make sure the oil is very hot but not smoking before you start cooking.

Raspberry Passion Fruit Swirls

This dessert is easy enough for even small children to make themselves.

Serves 4

INGREDIENTS
2 cups raspberries
2 passion fruit
1²⁄₃ cups fromage frais or strained
    plain yogurt
2 tbsp superfine sugar
raspberries and fresh mint sprigs,
    to decorate

passion fruit

raspberries

caster superfine sugar

fromage frais or strained plain yogurt

1 Mash the raspberries in a small bowl until the juice runs.

2 Scoop out the passion fruit pulp into a separate bowl with the fromage frais or yogurt. Sweeten with the sugar and mix well.

3 Place alternate spoonfuls of the raspberry pulp and the passion fruit mixture in stemmed glasses or one large serving dish.

4 Stir lightly to create a swirled effect. Decorate each dessert with a whole raspberry and a sprig of fresh mint. Serve chilled.

VARIATION
Other delicious fruit combinations would be raspberries with ripe peaches, or strawberries and mango. Drizzle the top with a little clear honey, if you like.

COOK'S TIP
Over-ripe, slightly soft fruit can be used in this recipe. Use frozen raspberries when fresh are not available, but thaw them first.

Carrot Cake

This is full of healthy fiber – yet moist
and soft and utterly irresistible.

Serves 10–12

INGREDIENTS
2 cups self-rising flour
2 tsp baking powder
scant 1 cup soft light brown sugar
$\frac{2}{3}$ cup ready-to-eat dried figs, roughly
    chopped
2 carrots, grated
2 small ripe bananas, mashed
2 eggs
$\frac{2}{3}$ cup sunflower oil
$\frac{3}{4}$ cup farmer's cheese
1$\frac{1}{2}$ cups confectioners' sugar, sifted
small colored candy, nuts or grated
    chocolate, to decorate

self-rising
flour

baking
powder

brown
sugar

dried figs

carrots

bananas

eggs

farmer's
cheese

sunflower
oil

confectioners'
sugar

1 Lightly grease an 7in round, loose-based springform cake pan. Cut a piece of baking parchment to fit the base of the tin, and place it in the tin.

2 Preheat the oven to 350°F. Put the flour, baking powder and brown sugar into a large bowl and mix well. Stir in the figs.

3 Using your hands, squeeze as much liquid out of the grated carrots as possible; add them to the bowl. Mix in the mashed bananas.

4 Beat the eggs and oil together and pour them into the mixture, beating well with a wooden spoon.

COOK'S TIP

Because this cake contains moist vegetables and fruit, it will not keep for longer than a week, but you probably won't find this a problem!

5 Spoon the mixture into the prepared pan and level the top. Cook for 1–1¼ hours, until a skewer pushed into the centre of the cake comes out clean. Remove the cake from the tin and leave to cool on a wire rack.

6 Beat the cream cheese and icing sugar together, to make a thick icing. Spread it over the top of the cake. Decorate with small colored candy, nuts or grated chocolate. Cut in small wedges to serve.

Blueberry Muffins

These monster muffins contain whole fresh blueberries that burst in the mouth when bitten. If your children do not like blueberries, try adding their favorite ingredient, or experiment with sultanas, raspberries or chocolate chips.

Makes 9

INGREDIENTS
3¼ cups all-purpose flour
scant 1 cup superfine sugar
1½ tbsp baking powder
1½ stick butter
1 egg, beaten, plus 1 egg yolk
⅔ cup milk
grated rind of 1 lemon
1½ cups fresh blueberries

flour

superfine sugar

baking powder

butter

egg yolk

egg

milk

lemon

blueberries

COOK'S TIP
The secret of successful muffins is to mix the dough lightly so it's best to do it by hand. If it is over-worked the muffins are liable to be tough.

1 Preheat the oven to 400°F. Line a muffin pan with nine large paper muffin cases.

2 Put the flour, caster sugar, baking powder and butter, cut into cubes, in a bowl. Rub in the butter until the mixture resembles fine breadcrumbs.

3 In a separate bowl, beat the egg, egg yolk, milk and lemon rind together well.

4 Pour the egg and milk mixture into the flour mixture, add the blueberries and mix gently together.

5 Divide the mixture among the cake cases and cook for 30–40 minutes, until they are risen and brown.

6 Gently push a skewer into the middle of a muffin to check that they are cooked. Cool on a wire rack.

Strawberry Apple Tart

Oats give this pastry a delicious nutty taste, while the fruity filling is juicy and full of flavor.

Serves 4–6

INGREDIENTS
1¼ cups self-rising flour
½ stick butter
⅔ cup rolled oats
2 cooking apples
2 cups strawberries, halved
¼ cup superfine sugar
1 tbsp cornstarch

self-rising flour

margarine

rolled oats

cooking apples

strawberries

superfine sugar

cornstarch

1 Preheat the oven to 400°F. Put the flour in a bowl and blend in the butter until the mixture resembles breadcrumbs. Stir in the oats, then add just enough cold water to bind the mixture to a firm dough. Knead lightly until smooth.

2 Roll out the pastry and line a 9in loose-based flan pan. Trim the edges, prick the base and line with baking parchment and the ceramic baking beans. Roll out the pastry trimmings and stamp out heart shapes using a cutter.

3 Bake the pastry case for 10 minutes, remove the paper and beans and bake for 10–15 minutes more or until golden brown. Bake the hearts until golden.

4 Peel, core and slice the apples. Place in a pan with the strawberries, sugar and cornstarch. Cover and cook gently, stirring, until the fruit is just tender. Spoon into the pastry case and decorate with the pastry hearts.

COOK'S TIP

Ceramic baking beans are useful when baking pastry blind, but ordinary dried beans work just as well. After use, cool them and store them in a jar clearly marked 'baking beans'. Just don't try cooking them!

Date Crunch

It's a date – next time your children invite half the neighborhood to tea, treat them to this tasty bake.

Makes 24 pieces

INGREDIENTS
8oz packet graham crackers
½ cup pitted dates
¾ stick butter
2 tbsp light corn syrup
½ cup golden raisins
5oz milk or bittersweet chocolate,
    broken into squares

graham crackers

dates

butter

light corn syrup

golden raisins

chocolate

1 Line an 7in sandwich pan with foil. Put the graham crackers in a plastic bag and crush them roughly with a rolling pin. Finely chop the dates.

2 Gently heat the butter and syrup in a small pan, stirring occasionally, until the butter has melted.

3 Stir in the crushed crackers, the dates and the golden raisins; mix well. Spoon into the tin, press flat with the back of a spoon and chill for 1 hour.

4 Melt the chocolate in a heatproof bowl over hot water, then spoon over the biscuit mixture, spreading evenly with a metal spatula. Chill until set, then lift the foil out of the tin and peel it away. Cut into 24 pieces and arrange on a plate.

VARIATION

For an alternative topping drizzle 3oz melted white and 3oz melted bittersweet chocolate over the mixture to give random squiggly lines. Chill until set.

COOK'S TIP

Take care not to break the plastic bag while you are crushing the crackers, otherwise the crumbs will fly out. You could try wrapping the bag in a dish towel as protection.

Gingerbread Jungle

Here's a recipe the children will enjoy following themselves. Just make sure they are supervised when using the stove or oven.

Makes 14

INGREDIENTS
1½ cups self-rising flour
½ tsp baking soda
½ tsp ground cinnamon
2 tsp superfine sugar
½ stick butter
3 tbsp light corn syrup
oil, for greasing
½ cup confectioners' sugar
1–2 tsp water

self-rising flour

baking soda

cinnamon

superfine sugar

butter

confectioners' sugar

light corn syrup

oil

VARIATION

These look like traditional gingerbread cookies, although the ginger has in fact been omitted to create a more subtle flavor.

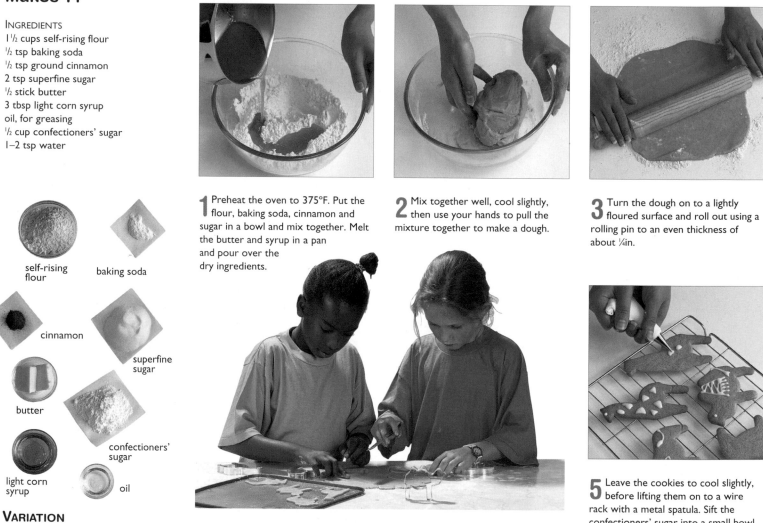

1 Preheat the oven to 375°F. Put the flour, baking soda, cinnamon and sugar in a bowl and mix together. Melt the butter and syrup in a pan and pour over the dry ingredients.

2 Mix together well, cool slightly, then use your hands to pull the mixture together to make a dough.

3 Turn the dough on to a lightly floured surface and roll out using a rolling pin to an even thickness of about ¼in.

4 Use animal cutters to cut shapes from the dough and space them on two lightly oiled baking sheets. Press the trimmings back into a ball, roll it out and cut more shapes. Continue to do this until the dough is used up. Cook the cookies for 8–12 minutes, until lightly browned.

5 Leave the cookies to cool slightly, before lifting them on to a wire rack with a metal spatula. Sift the confectioners' sugar into a small bowl and add enough water to make a fairly soft icing. Put the icing in a pastry bag fitted with a small plain nozzle and pipe decorations on the cookies.

Strawberry Smoothie and Starbursts

There's nothing more satisfying than a real strawberry smoothie, especially when it is served with crunchy cookies that are bursting with flavor. Great on a summer's day!

Serves 4–6

INGREDIENTS
FOR THE STRAWBERRY SMOOTHIE
2 cups strawberries
²⁄₃ cup strained plain yogurt
2 cups ice-cold milk
2 tbsp confectioners' sugar

FOR THE COOKIES
½ cup butter, roughly chopped
1½ cups all-purpose flour
¼ cup superfine sugar
2 tbsp light corn syrup
2 tbsp preserving sugar

strawberries

strained plain yogurt

milk

confectioners' sugar

butter

flour

light corn syrup

preserving sugar

superfine sugar

1 First make the star cookies. Put the butter, flour and superfine sugar in a bowl and rub until the mixture looks like breadcrumbs. Knead together to make a ball. Wrap in plastic wrap and chill in the refrigerator for 30 minutes.

2 Preheat the oven to 350°F. Lightly grease two baking sheets. Roll out the dough on a floured surface to a thickness of ¼in and use a 3in star-shaped cutter to stamp out the cookies.

3 Arrange the cookies on a baking sheet, leaving enough room for them to rise. Press the trimmings together and keep rolling out and cutting more cookies until all the mixture has been used. Bake for 10–15 minutes, until they are golden brown.

4 Put the syrup in a small heatproof bowl and heat it for 1–2 minutes over simmering water. Brush over the cookies while they are still warm. Sprinkle a little preserving sugar on top of each one and leave to cool.

5 To make the strawberry smoothies, reserve a few of the strawberries for decoration and put the rest in a blender with the yogurt. Whizz until fairly smooth.

6 Add the milk and confectioners' sugar, process again and pour into glasses. Serve each glass decorated with one or two of the reserved strawberries.

Hot Chocolate and Choc-tipped Cookies

For top spot in the parents' popularity poll, simply serve this winning combination. A steaming hot drink, and delicious choc-tipped cookies.

Serves 4

INGREDIENTS
FOR THE COOKIES
½ cup soft margarine
3 tbsp confectioners' sugar
1¼ cups all-purpose flour
few drops of pure vanilla extract
3oz semisweet chocolate, broken
    into squares

FOR THE HOT CHOCOLATE
6 tbsp drinking chocolate powder,
    plus extra for sprinkling
2 tbsp sugar
2½ cups milk
2 large squirts aerosol cream (optional)

margarine

confectioners'
sugar
flour

drinking
chocolate
powder

vanilla
extract
semisweet
chocolate

sugar

milk

1 Start by making the choc-tipped cookies. Put the margarine and confectioners' sugar in a bowl and beat them together until very soft. Mix in the flour and vanilla extract. Preheat the oven to 350°F and lightly grease two baking sheets.

COOK'S TIP
Make round cookies if you prefer, or cookies of any shape and dip half of each cookie in melted chocolate in the same way.

2 Put the mixture in a large pastry bag fitted with a star nozzle and pipe 4–5in lines on the baking sheets. Cook for 15–20 minutes, until pale golden brown. Allow to cool slightly before placing the cookies on to a wire rack. Leave the cookies to cool completely.

3 Put the chocolate in a small heatproof bowl. Place over a pan of hot, but not boiling, water and leave to melt. Dip both ends of each cookie in the chocolate, put back on the rack and leave to set.

4 To make the drinking chocolate, put the drinking chocolate powder and the sugar in a pan. Add the milk and bring it to the boil, whisking all the time. Divide between two mugs. Add more sugar if needed. Top with a squirt of cream, if you like.